STABLE

A Therapist and the Healing Nature of Horses

Emily Swisher

The cataloguing-in-publication is on file at the Library of Congress

Library of Congress Control Number: 2024906763

LCCN: 2024906763 ISBN: 9798321154281

First Edition Published 2024

This is a work of non-fiction, inspired by real-life stories and events. For the sake of confidentiality and respect to individuals mentioned, any identifying information has been altered, and in some scenarios, multiple accounts were combined into one character.

At the time of printing, the accepted terminology for this profession is considered psychotherapy incorporating equine interactions, but I have used equine therapy or equine psychotherapy for the sake of brevity.

For my family and friends,
both two-legged and four-legged.

"No philosophers so thoroughly comprehend us as dogs and horses."

—Herman Melville

CONTENTS

Introduction

The late-summer sun sent long shadows of the pine forest stretching across the shorn hay fields as it dipped below the ridge. Riding alongside my client on our evening trail ride, the progression of our horses scattered a herd of fifty or so whitetail deer, who alternated between grazing or bounding away, their heads raised at the audacity of our intrusion. The wide river below sent its damp smell mixing with the earthy dankness of the forest, its chill reminding us that the sun would soon retreat further to the south where the stillness of winter would encase this northern climate for the next eight months. The summer months in Montana are bright and brief and evenings such as this are savored for all of its golden richness.

I reflected on how the evening ride felt both surreal and bittersweet. I rode alongside a girl who was in many ways a younger version of myself. By age nine, she was already burdened with an enormous heart that struggled with finding a sense of belonging among her peers, but found solace with horses. It was from those same early roots that eventually led me to Montana, to this ranch providing psychotherapy incorporating horses to a small community that I adored. I never wanted the sweetness of this moment to end. Much like the ebbing and flowing herd of deer, thoughts of my future, where I wanted to settle or what next venture I wanted to pursue, were constantly moving and shifting. The horse-obsessed young girl in me had fulfilled her childhood fantasy of working on a horse ranch in Montana. Dreams are not necessarily tangible to be held in your hand and kept, but more fluid, always evolving. My heart was torn between the familiarity of the high-desert mountains back in Colorado, longing for the warmth of its intense sun, and the tranquil life I found for myself in northwest Montana, where the absence of that sun in winter could freeze deep enough into one's hope. Like turning a coin over in my hand, I had spent the last three years debating this potential move, eyeing both sides and weighing the pros and cons of each option. I often wondered whether I had pursued a childhood dream in Montana or had run away from a painful past, eager for a change of scenery. I felt myself paused as if hesitating at the confluence of a splitting river, much like the one my client and I were tracing on horseback, yet unable to decide which branch to follow. Closing my eyes, I focused on the swaying rhythm of the horse's movement beneath me. I felt my hips rock with each long-legged step the mare took, her head bobbing, staying alert with the surroundings, giddy with the mysteriousness that this time of dusk provided as other animals of the forest became more active. Brushing aside my uncertainties, I smiled knowing that as long as I could hear hoof beats, I would feel at home wherever I settled.

Blinking my eyes back open, I gazed out across the hay fields, where I had walked countless hours with clients plucking lone eagle feathers, sun-bleached deer bones and wildflowers from the ground together while mulling over heartache, conflicts and uncertainties. Finding solace in the western landscape and sharing that same groundedness I felt with horses from an early age with others truly felt like my calling. On my best days, I felt fortunate beyond measure that I'd found a profession where I was able to play and connect heart-to-heart with others in the beauty of the Rocky Mountains. But for every idyllic day, there were a dozen that brought frozen fingers and toes, trudging through snow and mud, sunburns and exhaustion, aching feet and joints. Yet I wouldn't trade a moment of it.

The healing power of horses has been felt globally by humans for centuries, dating back to ancient Greece, with Hippocrates proclaiming its benefits. It's only within the past three decades that this knowledge has been harnessed as a form

13

of therapy in itself. While I was confident in using horses for healing in my profession, it is said that a therapist can only take you as far as they themselves have gone. Despite many years and unknown circumstances awaiting me, I find meaning with what I have already endured as a way to better empathize with my therapy clients in their own stories. I use those experiences of pain or uncertainty to guide a client on their journey, normalizing their emotions, while offering encouragement that they too will find a sense of meaning in their tribulations. I like to imagine that younger self who drew blueprints of a ranch in Montana, a land I had yet to actually visit, but grew larger and more fantastical for me as a kid, would be proud of where I ended up. The journey from an impassioned young horse girl to a therapist integrating horses in psychotherapy, however, wasn't linear. The two-and-a-half decades in between included sudden relocations, breakups and setbacks, struggles with feelings of worthiness and self-destructiveness. Not to mention several wrong turns. But the idea of working alongside horses has continually nudged and whispered reassurances that guided my vocation and sense of belonging to something much larger than myself.

Sensing the growing silence between myself and my client, I pulled myself back into the moment. I asked her if she wanted to canter our horses back to the barn, already knowing the answer. Her freckled nose scrunched into a smile, her blue eyes glistening with daring determination. A gifted rider, she simultaneously gathered her reins shorter and alerted the horse to our intentions by shifting in her saddle and hugging her heels into her painted horse's sides. Our horses mirrored the same happiness and unbridled joy of running through a field together, four hearts playing in the freedom of the moment.

With the last golden rays of sun at our backs, we eased our horses back to a walk as we approached the barn. In a moment, we will be greeted by the happy yips and wagging tails of cattle dogs, the smiling faces of our friends caught in the same momentary bliss as they tacked their horses tethered to the barn, before setting out on their own evening ride. However fleeting moments like this exist in our world today, they are necessary and vital to our well-being. My only wish is to extend a glimpse into this private and sacred space, that the wisdom of horses can reverberate a bit further, reigniting something dormant in each of our hearts.

I hope by sharing these following stories that you may recognize pieces of yourself or of a loved one in these experiences. Each story was carefully selected to reveal a greater theme woven throughout our shared humanity.

1.

Grounding

Despite being pulled and shaped by varying influences at times, I'm fortunate in that I've never fully outgrown being the horse girl. There have been long phases where I prioritized other passions or strayed from the path, but that magical, unspoken human-equine language of Equus has patiently guided me along each step of my journey, serving as a foundation to center me if I stray too far from myself. I've learned many lessons from horses, spanning from the importance of work ethic, empathy and humility to standing my ground. In my professional role, I serve to translate these lessons to connect with clients who may be struggling with self-awareness, grief, communication or self-esteem.

Working with horses is just one transformational outlet, serving to reconnect us to nature and, ultimately, ourselves. Communicating non-verbally and through touch, clients can gain profound insight into themselves; a neurodivergent child learns how to regulate his emotions and behaviors so he is no longer excluded from peer play or reprimanded in school. A woman healing from domestic violence learns how to assert herself effectively, without feeling guilty or ashamed for defining her emotional and physical boundaries. A neglected child passed through endless hands in the foster care system experiences unconditional love and acceptance for the very first time. Each encounter feels fulfilling, from providing a momentary sense of joy in someone's week to witnessing something more miraculous, having heard impacted adults speaking their first word from the back of a horse or watching a child confined to a wheelchair from chronic pain begin to run alongside her horse after a few weeks of sessions together. The initial magnetic pull that first drew me towards horses only strengthens, witnessing how that same sense of magic can play a pivotal role in someone else's healing.

While I don't remember the exact moment I became fascinated with horses, I know it evolved quickly and has been a piece of my heart and spirit ever since. When I was six my family moved into our new ranch-style home on the outskirts of Greeley, a mid-sized farming town in northern Colorado. My adventurous spirit and desire to be outside all day blossomed with the new space and land surrounding us. With the Rocky Mountains looming on the horizon, I was never far from the wildness or serenity that nature provided. The snowmelt from those peaks accumulated during its descent to our agricultural community, the braiding rivulets settling in the sleepy Platte River, with fingers reaching out into the arid plains. Our three-acre yard, carpeted with thick grass and towering cottonwood trees and blue spruces, provided the perfect setting for building forts and inventing adventures. I built hidden worlds under the branches of those enormous spruces, scraped my hands and knees climbing them, and dug little fire pits around the yard, easily soothed and entertained by the landscape of the Front Range. As a kid who preferred to be outside and often alone, I was content to create and explore my own worlds in silence. The youngest of three siblings with a fairly large age gap, with parents who worked full-time, I was frequently left to my own devices to keep myself occupied throughout the afternoons after school and on weekends. Lucy, our chocolate Labrador, kept a passive eye on me as she sniffed the perimeter of our yard before inevitably being integrated into one of the stories I imagined for us; pioneers settling their homesteads or running around like Native Americans racing on horseback.

Nearing the turn of the millennium, I was occupied like other kids my age with Beanie Babies, listening to the Spice Girls and watching Cartoon Network. My true entertainment though, always came from the world outside my window. On one particular late-spring day, when the heat of the afternoon created a restlessness that led me to seek new excitement, I left the fenced perimeter of our yard towards our neighbor's property, which was home to several horses and a dozen or so goats. I fed the goats fistfuls of grass through the metal wire fence, entertained by the little mouths that tickled my fingers searching for more. I imagined feeling like a beloved diplomat, bestowing the gifts of leafy grasses equally to the crowd of goats who pushed and shoved each other along the fence line as my hands tore at more grass. Their cloven hooves balanced on the thin wire, allowing their necks to stretch upwards above their peers, hopeful for a bite. The sound of the tiny hooves on the loose wiring stapled to the worn, grey fence boards alerted the horses to new activity, their heads raised, assessing the intrusion. Eventually their curiosity and desire for their share of long grass lead them plodding over to the fence, sending the goats scrambling. I like to believe that first exhale of warm breath on my hand as the horse stretched its head towards me in curiosity was when the horse blew new life into me.

At first, I visited the horses infrequently, occupied by friends and other hobbies. But my attention became increasingly drawn from our manicured lawn to the untamed pasture grasses over the fence. I can still remember the footfalls of my route leading to the neighbor's property; slamming the front door and running along the side of our brick house, over the stepping stones between the tall, scrubby brushes. Terrified of seeing or stepping on a garter snake that frequently warmed themselves on those large, flat stones, I ran as fast as I could, setting my eyes straight ahead on the gate that marked the end of our property. It didn't take long before my dad had to replace that gate, after the weight of constantly climbing over it toppled the worn hinges from the wood-rotted post. With the newly installed gate slapping closed behind me, I was already preparing to duck between the middle and bottom boards of the pasture fence. Running up the final stretch of the neighbor's hill with the long grass whipping at my ankles, I'd feel my heart pounding in my chest, triumphant with speed.

At the crest of this hill, where the horses were housed in their paddocks, was also where the sprawling view of the mountains came into focus. My worn tennis shoes, windbreaker and messy wavy hair reflected the tomboy demeanor I exuded during these years; prioritizing comfort and practicality over any sense of style. The horses would be watching me amused, their eyes wide and ears pricked forward. Eventually one of the braver ones would approach for closer inspection. My hands and fingers would hungrily reach for whatever amount of contact with the horse's soft nose or shoulder I was granted, before it lost interest and sauntered away. Their sheer size sent my heart into rapture.

Despite being an animal lover, I had rarely interacted with horses before and knew almost nothing about them.

I quickly learned that unlike our dog Lucy, their attention was conditional. I was confused when they would simply twitch their tail and turn away from me lacking the same enthusiasm they had only moments earlier. The energy in their gait felt momentous as they had drawn towards me and I wondered how I could keep their attention. Pulling grass from the field around me, I'd extend the fistful as a desperate bribe for a horse to approach again. But there were times even when this didn't guarantee their acceptance to interact with me. Dejected, I'd watch as they swept the dusty paddock with their upper lip, searching for something and nothing all at the same time. On sunny days, the horses usually stood in one place snoozing with their eyelids closed and lower lip drooping. They were nothing like the exuberant stallions I'd seen rearing and racing around in movies.

While observing the horses wasn't as eventful as I'd imagined, I returned day after day to my new private world. My presence didn't go unnoticed for long. I was soon introduced to the owners who graciously tolerated my constant surveillance and questioning. Julia and Steve Grose, both older professionals with teenage kids, taught me all the horses' names and their relationships to one another. There was Johnny Boy, a tall, light bay thoroughbred gelding with a striking white blaze down the center of his face. He was a younger horse they had recently bought from a short-lived racing career and were training him for pleasure riding and jumping. Ebony was a dark bay filly, with a wild and spirited temperament. I rarely approached the young horse, her high energy was erratic and made me nervous. Her mother Susie Q, a flea-bitten grey Arabian, was the matriarch of the evolving herd. Her kind and soft energy was very inviting and safe, an easy introduction to the horse.

Like any great mentor, the Groses were patient and included me in their chores caring for the horses. For months I never missed a day or opportunity for Julia or Steve to introduce me to something new during their chores: scooping portions of grain with a rusted coffee can; tossing flakes of hay; grooming or cleaning stalls and dumping the full wheelbarrows in a pile at the bottom of the pasture.

Over dinner I would share everything I was learning with my family. Suddenly the quiet youngest child couldn't stop talking about horses. My parents listened patiently and I enthusiastically persuaded them to come visit the horses with me as soon as possible. Towing my parents behind, they met the Groses. When they offered me a ride that afternoon, I nearly fell over with the shock of happiness. Running home as fast as my legs could take me, I changed into jeans and dusted off a bike helmet from the garage; the closest thing I had to riding attire. Later, standing by the fence for instruction, I tried to appear calm and confident, but inside I felt my heart pounding with anticipation. I know that the first time they offered to lead me around the pasture on Susie Q's back my fate as a horse girl was sealed. What a gift it was to be offered a seat from the horse's perspective. It undoubtedly changed the trajectory of my life.

Now in my work with therapy clients, I can spot the exuberance of the 'horse girl' a mile away; the riding attire slowly accumulating over the months, growing from muck boots to riding breeches to paddock boots. Their parents scrounge local thrift stores and the internet for used boots and riding pants as their child grows like a wild weed overnight. I can feel the same anticipation in their chests as they pull out to the ranch and greet the horses for the very first time; always sure to impress me by having remembered all the names of the herd members by the next time we meet. Their parents typically sought me out for their children who have been described as sensitive, grappling with expressing emotions appropriately, while all sharing the common preference of spending time alone with animals. Perhaps that is why we are continually drawn back to the quiet mysteries of the barn. Our heart and spirit are met by others who don't share our language, but can only communicate through mutual respect, untethered by social constraints.

Even for those who don't share the same enthusiasm as horse lovers, horses are a refuge for those who wear their heart on their sleeve in a world where we're taught to keep our cards close to our chest, trying to interpret others' motives before we play our next hand. What a relief it can be to find sanctuary where our hearts can breathe fully without fear.

My newfound interest in horses as a kid didn't escape the attention of my family as I began collecting anything I could related to horses. A collage of trail-riding brochures and photos carefully cut from magazines grew on my cork board, as I circulated through the school library books on equines and their care. I bought my first toy horse after my summer soccer season one afternoon; a dark-brown Barbie figurine with outlandishly large green eyes, complete with a glittery plastic saddle and bridle. Something about the toy's exaggerated features felt disappointing though. The beauty and wildness of horses needs no embellishment. As my interest continued with momentum, we were able to find more authentic-looking figures and books that helped me understand the complexity of how many variations of horses there could be, yet my curiosity was still not satiated. During the summer, I pleaded with my parents to drive the hour to Estes Park, where trail-riding outposts tailored to floods of tourists as the only direct access to horses I had at that time.

I began saving money with my best friend Dakota for a horse to share, our crumpled bills and spare change growing in the bottom of an old pickle jar. With our nine-year-old logic, we concluded that our thousand-dollar goal would be sufficient to buy and maintain a horse. Factors such as breed, age, temperament, discipline didn't even cross our minds. A horse was a horse and we were just determined to get close to one. Dakota's family had a large pasture, overgrown with tall weeds, and a stable currently housing only mice that would provide an appropriate home, or so we thought. Inevitably, this plan, like many childhood dreams, was short-lived before our funds were separated and we returned to our other games around the neighborhood.

Never deterred, I grabbed copies of the local newspaper, *The Greeley Tribune*, after my parents had skimmed through them, so that I could scan the classifieds section to learn more about buying a horse. Somewhere tucked between ads of 'Border Collie Puppies for Sale' and used farming equipment, I would find cryptic listings such as: *14 y.o. Chestnut QH Mare. Dead broke, good trail companion or husband horse. Good home only $2,000 OBO.*

The complexity of horse purchasing and ownership only compounded when I discovered websites on our dial-up internet, which were solely devoted to selling and leasing performance horses. Suddenly I could filter based upon color, discipline, location—essentially creating a perfect horse. Late at night at sleepovers with friends, our faces would glow eagerly in the blue haze from the computer screen as we scrolled through photos and listings for horses across the country. On occasion we'd print out our 'dream horse' profile, determined to wish hard enough about owning something so magnificent one day. Bonded with the two other horse girls at my elementary school, our weekends were filled by hours of playing with our Breyer horse models, hauled over to one another's homes in duffle bags, with our pajamas and a toothbrush shoved deep in a side pocket as an afterthought. Every minute was consumed by the thought of horses and we found refuge in one another.

While our parents tolerated our horse-obsessed sleepovers and our teachers may have rolled their eyes when every assignment was somehow connected to a horse or horse theme, our peers weren't as understanding when our fantasies spilled over into the school week and onto the playground. Looking back, I can see how pawing at the ground on all fours or running around in a bouncy canter as if we were riding horses was an easy target for bullies. I don't think it ever bothered us much. In time we learned some things were meant to be shared in the privacy of our rooms and backyards, while other games and entertainment were more socially acceptable for the playground.

I like to believe that our pre-adolescent selves were the ultimate expert of our happiness, before we became disenchanted from peer influence and worried about standing out. Each of us deals with it differently, yet we never share the grief we all experience leaving childhood as we move into adolescence. It is a slow and unspoken process. Once that shift sets in, we began looking at our dolls, plastic horses and toys in a new light. We loved them simply and dearly, but we created distance from anything that could be seen as childish. Pop culture, fashion, makeup and the opposite sex became our new obsessions, yet they felt so intimidating and awkward. We may have attempted to wear the right clothes or use the right slang, but they hung on us like an ill-fitting costume on an actor. Then there were days when keeping up with our peers was so discouraging that we closed our bedroom doors, pulled out the closeted toys and soothed ourselves with mementos of a simpler past.

If we're lucky enough, or one of the brave few who cling to the passions, lessons and relationships of our upbringing, we can remain somewhat shielded from the distracting influence of our culture. Our passions are always to be carried in our hearts, urging us to reconsider the pressure of conformity. In our younger innocence, we were drawn towards our interests solely by the feeling that it brought us happiness. They were the simplest barometer to our wellbeing and identity. If we stray from these passions for long, they urge, nudging us back, if only we listen.

I find joy in asking therapy clients in my office what they enjoyed playing as a child, where their imagination led them. It takes a moment for the adults to reflect back, before an inevitable smile spreads across their face and they share their stories, almost as if it were a secret. I hear how they used their younger siblings to stage performances for their parents, play rescuer as they saved others from peril or gathered the neighborhood kids for large games of Red Rover or street hockey. Tying that into their current life, I weave in how their interest in justice and being a hero led to their career in the military or creating performances aided in the creativity they use as an event planner. Conversely, we also look for the ways those passions are absent in their lives—how can they invite that creativity and play back in. Finding ways to reconnect with our younger imaginative play is a gift for ourselves and to those around us.

Every single one of us has a gift that is worthy of being shared, unique to ourselves and our journey. My own has grown from the roots of an impassioned young horse girl through heartaches and triumphs that continue to draw me closer and closer to some of the stories my clients share in therapy. I have carried these experiences close to my heart, in awe of the beauty of connection between people, animals, the land and something much larger than ourselves. What a blessing it is to be an observer into the human experience.

2.

A New Language

Before I began using horses in psychotherapy sessions, I started teaching adaptive riding lessons for children and adults with differing physical or cognitive abilities. Many of these riders were either limited in verbal expression or completely non-verbal. During our lessons, we would instill the practice that if capable, the rider would signal for the horse to walk by saying, "Walk on" and to stop by calling "Whoa." Not only would this alert the person leading the horse, but it reinforced sequencing and impulse control for the rider. Most kids also happen to love calling the shots for a change.

Alex embodied the unbridled emotional spectrum as a seven-year-old with autism. His boundless joy reverberated in the bounce of his step, the blonde cowlick on the back of his head mirroring his springy toe walking. Every greeting was as if he was seeing someone he loved dearly after a long absence: "HELLO!" or "HI, TUFFY!" to his horse. Despite being limited to a handful of expressions at his age, his open-hearted

31

enthusiasm was difficult to misinterpret. Conversely, any small deviation to his schedule or environment could send him into a full-bodied tantrum, usually collapsing to the ground in a heap of tears. Fortunately, I'm gifted with the very special talent to mimic most farm animal calls that kids like Alex find irresistibly silly, but there were days when even the bleating of a sheep or quack of a duck could not redirect his mood. Defeated, his mom would concede to pulling him from the arena and trying again for our ride the following week.

It was clear which emotion Alex was feeling in each moment, cueing myself and the volunteers to reciprocate his enthusiasm, offer comfort when he was upset or set clear boundaries when his impulsive behavior was becoming a safety risk. Watching the huge smile light up on Alex's face while he grabbed the saddle horn for balance and with us jogging alongside his horse to urge it into a trot, it seemed cruel to ever ask a child to restrain their emotions to be more acceptable for society's standards. "Good JOB!" he would exclaim, clapping for all of us after we settled back into a walk, his toes pressing up on the stirrups to emphasize his point.

His joy was contagious, spreading through myself and the other volunteers during his lessons. Children and animals typically wear their emotions on their sleeve and it can be a gentle reminder to those of us who have learned to guard or protect our hearts. Most communication is non-verbal through facial expression or posture, and that extends into the animal world as well. Those non-verbal expressions can be the most beautiful moments to share with one another, knowing the same feelings are passing between us. The feeling of coming home to our much-relieved pets or laughing along with our closest best friend are universal. At times when the outside world can feel a bit confusing, seeing that unmistakable joy in another can remind us how very loved we are simply for existing.

In equine therapy, I initially serve as a translator between the horse's non-verbal behavior to clients like Alex. Most of the activities I teach with horses involve working with them on the ground, the care and maintenance of grooming, effectiveness in leading and communication with body language. The client learns to make adjustment from reading the warning of a swishing tail or pinned ears, or to recognize the pleasure response of licking and chewing. By observing the horse, a client is learning to remain grounded in the present moment, recognizing their non-verbal behavior, as well as their internal emotions and physical sensations.

Whether with a person or a horse, each interaction starts with a greeting. Anticipating the urge to reach out towards an animal's face, I will instead show a client how to properly greet a horse with a handshake. Instructing them to make a soft fist and extending it out towards the horse's face, the client will experience how the horse reciprocates this greeting by extending their nose to exhale on the back of their hand. Even when my clients progress to riding, that routine is still ingrained as a foundation of care and building an ongoing relationship with a horse. In wishing for the privilege of riding, we must always be ready to offer our respect for what the horse is communicating as well.

My fascination with horses continued to grow as I navigated through the awkward pre-adolescent years towards the finality of elementary school. I began to recognize and find immense pleasure in hearing the throaty whicker that the horses made when I climbed the hill to greet them each day. Acting like a patient ecologist, I started taking notes of my observations in a notebook while I sat watching from the goat shed. I noted how the horses extended their front teeth to clip at the short grasses or how they showed affection through mutual grooming. Standing lengthwise facing opposite directions, two horses will curve their necks over one another's backs and use their teeth and lips to scratch and nuzzle one another. I observed their curious behavior, but had no way of interpreting it.

At home, I began collecting real-estate ads for land in Montana listed in the back of magazines or cutting out ads for stall doors and tractor equipment from *Horse Illustrated*; anything I thought my horse ranch may need one day. I stuffed these clippings in a manila envelope and dreamed of a future surrounded by mountains, horses, and others who were drawn to them as well. In sketchbooks, I would draw aerial maps of the future property; plotting homes, stables, a veterinary clinic and a wild horse herd at different intervals. No aspect of the dream seemed unreasonable.

On the evening of my tenth birthday, the phone rang in my bedroom. We had all just finished dinner and with my parents watching from my bed, I answered the phone, hoping to sound very mature in my new age.

"Hi, is Mark available?" the woman asked.

Not recognizing her voice, I responded as if she were a telemarketer in the way my parents had instructed, "I'm sorry, he's not here right now."

"Oh, can you let him know this is Penny calling back about the horse?"

I imagine my eyes must have bulged out of my head with the shock of her words 'the horse.' I couldn't let this woman hang up, so I stammered something quickly, "Oh, actually he's right here!" I shoved the cordless phone into my dad's hands and eagerly watched his expression as he finished the conversation with the woman.

Smiling, he hung up the phone and paused for effect. "Well..." I held my breath as he explained we would go visit some stables where a woman had advertised a horse for lease that following weekend.

My bed was stacked with stuffed horses, drawers overflowed with T-shirts with horse silhouettes and a toy barn full of Breyer horse models filled the floor space in my room. It couldn't be ignored that this obsession was here to stay. With an older sister focused on dance and a brother involved in soccer and track, my parents were wading into unfamiliar territory with the horse-obsessed daughter. I knew the decision to add a horse to our lives had been weighed heavily between the two of them behind closed doors. My face and heart beamed with love and joy that evening. I felt wholly seen and loved.

Redwind was a slightly overweight chestnut Morgan horse with a flaxen mane and tail, a white sock on his hind foot and a white blaze down the front of his face. Penny struggled to get the leather headcollar of the bridle over Redwind's ears while my dad and I watched, explaining that it had always been difficult to do with him raising his head in defiance. His resistance, paired with his tail that hung lopped to one side, I would later find out that he had suffered abuse at the hands of someone who had pulled his tail until it had broken, letting it heal crooked, and twisted his ears to force him to drop his head during bridling to make it easier on the handler. Those cruel tactics were sadly too common with handlers that weren't patient enough with proper training, justifying their ignorance with the mentality that horses were just dumb animals meant to be manhandled and restrained into compliance. Despite his quirks and neglected appearance, all I saw in front of me was the most beautiful horse in the world.

Arthritis in his hind hip caused a hitch in his gait, his crooked tail bobbing along as we led him to the outdoor arena. Expecting me to have had some riding experience, Penny turned Redwind and I free into the arena, while she stood outside the white fence with my dad to watch our trial ride. Having only gone on supervised trail rides in Estes Park with dead-broke horses, I really didn't know how to actually ride, but I didn't want to embarrass myself in front of Penny. How hard could it be?

Lifting my hands on the reins and pressing my heels into his side, I urged the chestnut horse into a trot and for 30 seconds it was complete bliss. The horse trotted, zig-zagging across the arena and I giggled with the delight and feeling of freedom, dreaming about my own horse. Picking up momentum, Redwind began to canter. I had never been in a canter before! It was every horse girl's fantasy to run free and uninhibited on the back of a horse.

What I didn't realize at the time was that Redwind was actually becoming irritable with me bouncing awkwardly on his back. With the flick of his head, he threw a buck that launched me up out of the saddle, over his left shoulder, and hard into the arena sand. Reeling from the impact and feeling of betrayal, I crawled onto my hands and knees, trying desperately not to cry as I heard my dad and Penny running up behind me. Penny apologized and ran to grab ahold of Redwind's dangling reins as the horse wandered back towards the gate while my dad helped me stand and brush the dirt off myself. Embarrassed, we all tried to move past it, making assurances to communicate soon, but I couldn't help but think that I had just blown my chance of having a horse.

Despite the chaos of my first ride, everyone miraculously agreed that I was responsible enough and ready to lease Redwind. Other than brief, backyard horses in their own childhoods, my parents had no experience with the actual care and maintenance of a horse as they worked to help me with chores and his handling. The other boarders at the stable watched us from the corner of their eyes as we struggled to bridle Redwind before our lessons, fed him fistfuls of treats and scraped together mismatched riding tack. A few made hints to my parents at my lack of arena etiquette, but eventually they softened when they saw how enamored we were, despite how amusing our lack of experience could be at times.

Redwind was kept at a stable near our home, the long dusty driveway lined with large cottonwood trees that gave some reprieve from the harsh sun that dried the plains before climbing towards the looming, brown steel indoor arena with stalls running the length of each side. There were two large outdoor arenas that could be guaranteed to be set with jump courses, while a full dressage court started on the expanse of the 300-acre cross-country course.

In order to start riding, Lindy, a local riding instructor, drove in for our lessons on Saturdays; her black Four Runner throwing up dust as she sped up the driveway, usually running significantly behind schedule. To continue to practice my riding throughout the week, she instructed my parents how to hold the lunge line clipped to Redwind's bridle, as I circled around them, learning to balance for the trot, my posting movements clumsy and irregular. Learning to ride the trot can be the most difficult aspect of riding. It's a two-beat rhythm that is hard to coordinate new muscle development and absorb the horse's movement while balancing on their back. Posting is a riding technique in which a rider uses the upward momentum of the trot to stand in the stirrups before briefly sitting down again, which is gentler on the horse's back and allows for more movement.

During those early rides with limited supervision, I took liberties jumping fences I wasn't supposed to or urged Redwind to gallop, crouching over his back like a jockey. He typically dumped me into the sand after each of these attempts, cheekily reinforcing his irritation and my ignorance. These painful and embarrassing falls quickly enforced that the freedom gained from riding a horse is a privilege, requiring patience, good judgment and respect for your horse. Skipping steps for the rider's benefit or amusement will inevitably result in an unhappy horse, or create an unsafe environment for the horse and rider. I surrendered to the slow but methodical progression of learning the foundations of riding. Soon we were trotting over cross rails as I held the crouched, two-point position of lifting my weight off the saddle and putting it down into my heels and stirrups that Lindy demonstrated, meant to balance yourself over the horse's neck while jumping.

With the responsibility of a horse in my life, I doubt that I ever complained about having to leave sleepovers early for a riding lesson. Although my friends might not have appreciated the earthy smell of the barn lingering on my clothes after showing up late to their birthday parties or playdates. I know that my parents made similar sacrifices in their schedules along with me as they shuttled me to and from the barn. I can remember one winter evening as I was getting ready for bed, a blizzard had rolled in unexpectedly and I tearfully pleaded with my dad to drive out to the barn to blanket Redwind. I was tortured by the idea of him shivering alone in his stall with the dropping temperature. Together my dad and I braved the storm, our car slowly creeping along the highway in low visibility as heavy snowflakes thrashed the windshield, illuminated by our headlights. Running through the snow to the barn, the horses were surprised by the aisle lights suddenly flickering on. I was reassured to see Redwind sleeping contently in his stall, but also secretly relieved to add the comfort of a warm blanket on him that night.

Much like being bucked off by Redwind into the arena sand, middle school had been a difficult transition for me. I was in need of a connection and space where I could feel free to be accepted for who I was. At age 11, my scrawny frame grew more gangly and stooped, my slumped shoulders and greasy bangs attempted to deflect any attention my way. I felt wholly inferior and flawed compared to the vivacious and curvy girls in my new school, not knowing how to mimic their unfamiliar slang and behavior. Starting sixth grade, I transferred to the only private school in our town, splitting from the rest of my larger friend group. The khaki pants and shapeless polos did little to help with my confidence and, with the entire sixth grade consisting of only 13 peers, it was easy to stand out. I missed the familiarity of my elementary school, my friends at recess. Like the clumsy and irregular rhythm of learning to ride, the transition into my teen years was anything but smooth.

Redwind didn't notice the particular animal emblem stitched into my polos, the pimples covering my forehead or the alternating-colored ties of my braces. I found peace in the solitude that horses offered in a world full of noise, always requesting more of you. In the evenings after school finishing my rides, I'd drop the girth and slide the sweaty pad and saddle from his back. Riding bareback out of the arena and into the long grasses, I could get lost staring at the mountains on the horizon while my mind spun around the new feelings and anxieties I was experiencing for the first time. I let Red grab mouthfuls of alfalfa as a reward between his strides, the bushy green grass speckled with purple flowers reaching past his knees. Sharing the silence with the evening summer skies before us dripping with color like a painting, Redwind offered acceptance at a time when I was feeling wildly out of place and struggling to belong.

Much like starting to compare myself to the other girls at school, I started noticing the older and more experienced riders at the barn; the different tack and riding aids they used. I wanted to blend in with their apparent confidence and started wearing spurs, without knowing if they were necessary or how to use them properly. With soaring hormones and insecurity, I began to use my riding stick much harder than necessary when I became frustrated by Red's lack of response, or rather my poor communication with him. I was conflicted and ashamed from using force with Red. My neighbor mentor, Steve, who also kept several horses at that boarding stable, would reassure me that my actions weren't being cruel, reasoning that "they make baseballs out of their hides." I would reflect on this statement many years later, as I watched the twitching flesh of horsehide dance as the tiny, delicate legs of flies tickled their skin. It is a limited life that underestimates the capacity of animals.

While I was battling new emotions and the reflection in the mirror, my family was undergoing massive changes as well. In addition to losing more consistency with friends when I transferred schools, my older brother Nathan had joined my sister Megan at college and I missed their company and guidance. My father also began commuting to California for a new job managing a printing manufacturing company, flying home to Colorado on the weekends. I was facing a transformative time fairly alone without much of a peer guide. Pre-adolescence is when the illusions of childhood begin to dissolve, dreams are met with practicalities and limitations. With the dissolution of childhood beliefs also comes a much broader world that we begin exploring and testing new boundaries.

Over those angsty teen years, I'd ride out onto the windswept prairie with Red. I thought that if I rode fast enough, I wouldn't be able to hear the whisperings of my parents discussing moving from Colorado. Feelings I couldn't express came out through the thrumming of my horse's hooves as my fists clenched tightly around the reins. My mom would attempt to follow along, trying to keep me within view, but my erratic emotions and anger towards my circumstances would encourage me to push my boundaries and ride further, wishing I could run to the wall of Rockies that had defined my view for so long. The tips of Mount Meeker and Longs Peak had always been like a honing device that ground me deeply to the landscape of Colorado. These two iconic peaks, seen from the northern Front Range, are showcased in the classic 'M' shape that a child might use to draw mountain peaks. Seen from further south in Denver, the two eclipse one another and look like a solid sloping mountain. Riding around in the backseat of our car, I'd always watch out the window for the two peaks to become separate; evidence of how close I was to home. Where would I be and who would I become if I could no longer see those peaks? From Red's back, I loved watching the light dance across the plains. Shafts of sunlight would illuminate from the clouds, combing themselves over the land, the dry rainstorms leaned over the plains like a curtain, shedding their tears.

Redwind was my companion and friend, who carried me and my secrets on the stillness of that great expanse. As I rode across the prairie at the barn, time stood still and the noise inside my head subsided. My only focus was the ground in front of us; navigating terrain, minding prairie dog holes and scouting the route that lay ahead. When everything else in my life felt out of my control, I knew in those fleeting, all-consuming moments I could at least control the animal beneath me. While I never neglected the routine and consistency in caring for Red, I had many years to go before I would learn about the emotional responsibility we owe to our horses. It extends much deeper than indulging them with treats and being consistent with their maintenance. Horsemanship is the art of putting our expectations aside to truly listen to what our horse is telling us each day, even if it was not what we were hopefully expecting.

Transitions between locations, schools, homes and life stages require new interpretation and language. We're forced to let go of familiar routines, while also remaining open with expectations for how the future will go. Without a strong guide, I misinterpreted Red's annoyance until I learned through painful lessons that my excitement to push boundaries was distressing him. As social herd animals, horses remind us to slow down and pay attention to how we are communicating with the world around us. Most often many of our interactions with other people are non-verbal and we make assumptions based on their unspoken emotions and intentions, leading to gaps of miscommunication. While the unbridled joy of clients like Alex can feel purely contagious, learning stronger social nuances can enable him to interact with a much larger world. I could've greatly benefited from a mentor during my angsty teenage years to help normalize my emotions or shift my perspective on the changes occurring in my life. Fortunately, Redwind offered forgiveness for days when I was emotional, tolerated when I pushed his boundaries and looked beyond my lack of horse care knowledge. In riding horses we borrow freedom, but we have much more to learn from the consistency, communication and empathy we learn in return.

3.

Fight, Flight, Freeze

Why horses? The intention behind using horses in psychotherapy sessions resides in the unique horse-human interaction, given horses are prey animals who survive in a herd dynamic, while humans are innately wired as predators. A horse's heightened nervous system is biologically designed to constantly scan and assess for threats in their environment. Any strange movement, noise or ominous behavior triggers their instinctual need to flee. It's not too dissimilar from how anxiety alerts our nervous system of potential threats and the need to react as humans. Instead of the circling pack of wolves, our nervous system is responding to constant stimulation from alerts and reminders, noise, mounting responsibilities, facing future uncertainties, advertisements and people around us. Horses may always flee from danger, but we respond to stressors in a variety of different ways, from the avoidance or resistance to acknowledging our emotions, fighting ourselves through negativity and risky behavior, and the learned helplessness of numbing from the reality around us.

Horses are just one way that we can find that groundedness in the present moment, releasing ourselves from the hypervigilance of fight, flight or freeze. In order for a horse to feel safe or relaxed in our presence, we first have to be congruent with our behavior and emotions. Horses are always seeking peace. It is wasted energy for horses (and people) to be hypervigilant to threats at all times, so they have to be discerning on what warrants the energy of running away or reacting quickly.

As a therapist, I will instruct a client to imagine the scene of a watering hole in the African savannah. Herds of elephants, zebra, wildebeests, antelope are all peacefully commingling, even appearing to be content with the big cats observing safely from a distance. The prey animals have evolved to be aware that big cats are only actively hunting and seeking prey roughly one or two hours a day; a slumbering pride of lions napping in the shade of a tree doesn't warrant a threat. Conversely, an alert pride of lions sitting up and scanning the herd intently as their pride members begin fanning out is something to take awareness of and potentially start alerting the other herd members.

Despite being domesticated for thousands of years, horses are still scanning for these nuances when they are interacting with us. Because horses are prey animals, they're constantly reading and reflecting the emotional intent of other beings around them. If we are attempting to catch them with a halter, but our energy and shoulders are raised with abrupt movements, they are going to feel threatened or concerned. This is what most people describe when they have heard stories of how horses 'know' a person's character. In reality, they are just mirroring how congruent we are in our bodies and the level of self-awareness we possess.

As their leader, if a horse senses anxious or fearful behavior from us, they believe we must know of a threat in the environment and begin to react as well. It is a misconception that we have to be brave or confident around a horse at all times, when we really just need to recognize and accept whatever emotion we are feeling. Suppressing an emotion with a brave face is the inconsistency that alerts a horse to something feeling wrong or 'off' about us. Horses will still engage with us and respond to our vulnerable feelings of sadness or nervousness as long as we own and accept them ourselves.

Those who have endured trauma or are more sensitive to the intentions of others can relate to those subtle shifts in behavior or mannerisms as a cause for concern. Someone who was raised with an alcoholic or violent parent is attuned to the delicate nuances in tone of voice or patterns of behavior long before the shouting, accusations or fists start flying.

Many of us have experienced feeling drained or depleted from interacting with certain people without having a logical way to describe *exactly* what aspect about that person was off-putting or uncomfortable. Horses remind us to trust our instincts, to listen to our gut, which is attempting to alert us of inconsistencies around us to consider for our own safety and wellbeing. And unlike humans, horses don't possess the societal pressures to feel obligated to spend time with a person or herd mate. It's not personal, it's survival to them. It can take many years for us as humans to learn to stop complying with obligations and relationships that are only damaging us emotionally.

One way that young women can especially become separated from their instinctual gut feeling, is the pressure to remain pleasant and kind. We were rewarded as young girls for being compliant, following instruction, completing our work and not adding any stress for our teachers or parents. Due to our more social and empathic nature, we are hypersensitive to how our actions impact others, which can serve many benefits being a part of a larger social and familial structure. However, it can become common to suppress our own needs and emotions by prioritizing everyone else's. This fear of hurting someone's feelings can be used manipulatively by partners or create pressure for a girl to comply, even when she feels uncomfortable.

Girls suffer the most during the transition from childhood into adulthood, as the transformation to our bodies is more apparent and we separate from one another and become more isolated from our friends and families. Without acknowledging it, we feel that our self-value is now contingent upon our bodies, how it may grow and shape as we move into womanhood. We envied our older siblings and schoolmates from afar, trying to emulate and copy their words, their behavior, their clothing. Their discarded hand-me-downs felt like treasure, as if the secret wisdom of this transformation would be passed down along with it. Seeking courage, we would ask our mother to buy the *Seventeen* magazine we had been eyeing for weeks. Articles would list the transformative beauty products and clothing we needed "for him to notice you." The mirror became our nemesis, as we attempted to copy hairstyles or makeup tricks from magazines and movies, before frustrated tears streaked down our cheeks and we studied our new reflection, picking at deficiencies we never previously noticed.

Then one day in middle school, a teacher or school nurse separated us from the boys in our class and the division began to set in like a rift between us. We learned how our bodies would suddenly become shameful and betray us as it began to change and grow. Zits erupted on our face, thick hair started growing in new places and this wounded body would bleed monthly creating a sense of embarrassment and shame. We hurt from being divided and isolated, our new insecurities provoked us to begin lashing out at ourselves and one another. We formed new alliances with peers based on social image and discarded reliable old friends if they impacted our delicate social status. Our passions and values were discarded along with them, attempting to create separation from our younger, child self. We shoved previously loved items, friendships, values and innocence into a closet, stuffing our shame along with it. This urge to separate and cleave ourselves from what was familiar left us lonely and vulnerable.

At the height of my pre-teen angst of eighth grade, the decision to move from Colorado was finalized between my parents and I spent the summer saying goodbye to friends and revisiting my favorite places, desperate to cling to their memories. That wall of mountains that had provided a sense of security for me throughout my childhood gave way into prairies, and then into the rolling hills of the Midwest, as we moved into the unfamiliar territory of St. Louis, Missouri. The new landscape also entailed navigating a new culture and social structure as well. Our Colorado home, tucked into an oasis with mountain views, was traded for a suburban neighborhood where larger homes were prioritized, stretching to fill the lot sizes, leaving little room for even a lawn or backyard that no one seemed to spend time in.

In addition to the lack of connection to nature, I remember immediately being struck by the racial prejudices my new peers flung around; terms and standards that I had a hard time deciphering their true meaning. Two boys, wanting to introduce me to the neighborhood, mentioned "the brown kid down the street." But they reassured me that he was a "county brownie," which I would later learn meant a black peer who lived in the county rather than being bused into the suburban schools from the city. Another neighbor girl walked me up the street, climbing the asphalt hill one afternoon, when she nodded casually towards a white colonial house and mentioned her parents "disapproved" of the family that lived there because their son had "married a black girl."

Starting high school in a strange new environment, I learned there was also an entirely new hierarchical structure I hadn't yet been exposed to, based on race and class with many clauses. I began to understand that neighborhoods, schools and suburbs were not only categorized by wealth, but by what type of wealth someone had: new money, old money, Jewish, educated or lucky.

Redwind, my Morgan horse, who had carried me to first place in eventing competitions throughout Colorado and Wyoming was denied boarding at a prestigious jumping barn because of his breed, or so they told us. Suddenly we were aware of being 'not good enough.' Standing out was dangerous and I began denying my inner voice and passions further to avoid drawing more attention towards myself. From that point on, status became an inexplicable burden that would continue to define me for years to come. In the riding world, horses have always welcomed me, it's the people who have judged based on my perceived value.

Fitting in with new standards, rules and culture was stressful, but I managed to find a small friend group who welcomed me. I became involved in theater and orchestra, while still riding Red after rehearsals three to four days each week as I always had. I kept him separate from the rest of my new world and I didn't attempt to get to know the other girls at the barn who went to different schools. He was the last remaining association I had to the western lifestyle I had been painfully removed from; sometimes it was easier to ignore him and that piece of me.

I began to feel slightly embarrassed about my connection to horses and it was inevitable that a boyfriend or my new friends would replace my time and attention away from my beloved horse. Red was well-cared-for and still brought me happiness, but he was no longer a priority in my life. I was trying to reinvent myself for approval and became hyper-fixated on my image and body. I can remember starting to stare down at my thighs in class, feeling ashamed for how large and bulging they looked sitting at my desk. The shame rolled in like a fog. I was consumed by self-loathing and comparing myself to popular girls at school or the curvy, hourglass-figured women I saw in magazines. With the loss of outdoor recreation, shopping malls became a new source of entertainment for me and my mom, while my dad focused on his new job and my older siblings remained living out west. The labels and ads suggested my ripped jeans and T-shirts were unbecoming and tacky. I tried on different clothes like I was seeking a new identity.

The summer of 2006 after my freshman year, our theater department had been invited to participate in the Edinburgh Fringe Festival in Scotland, one of the world's greatest arts festivals, a huge honor for high school thespians. I rehearsed excitedly with a group of friends over the summer leading up to our departure. Several parents and our theater director's close friend and younger brother acted as chaperones during our trip.

That August we flew to London, enjoying the tourist destinations we had only read about until then. Friendships and inside jokes grew like wildfire as we traveled north and began getting ready to perform. Craig, one of the chaperones, was like the fun older brother that I missed so much. He was sweet and silly, and soon the group began to look up to and admire him. Getting Craig's approval or attention was riveting. He was slightly stocky with short brown hair and brown eyes, but the girls found him handsome in a sweet, unconventional way. Craig was novel and new, and being abroad away from the supervision of my parents allowed some freedom to begin experimenting with being flirtatious. I was still used to being the funny friend in my close circle, but mostly unnoticed to the larger social cliques at school. Somehow despite that, Craig noticed me and we began joking with one another and seeking individual attention. Having always been the gangly, awkward girl that most guys my age didn't seem to find attractive, I felt so mature and even unique to have caught the eye of an older guy. While our entire trip only lasted ten days, my interactions with Craig escalated after several days in Scotland. He suggested that we separate from the group and go on a hike together to Arthur's Seat, a grassy knoll on a wild, rugged hillside outside of Edinburgh, where he kissed me. I had just turned 15 and he was 22. I had never been in a relationship, with the exception of a few bashful middle-school boyfriends that never progressed into much. It felt exciting and the attention he gave me felt genuine and sweet. I would later learn how predators groom their prey in ways to make them feel validated and unique. Often for young women it is simply attention in feeling seen and loved.

Only a day or two later, Craig snuck me into the boy's dorm on the university campus, where we were staying, and urged me to perform oral sex on him. I remember being slightly scared, my heart pounding, as I tried to act calm and cool. I had never seen a penis before and had no idea what I was doing. After returning to my own dorm with the other girls, I had the sudden impulsion to use my shaving razor and began making superficial cuts on my arms and thighs. I wouldn't see the connection in timing of my first sexual experience with my first urges to self-harm and inflict pain on myself for many more years.

At 15, I didn't have the context or the language to understand of what had happened or, more specifically, what was happening to me. Fifteen is a completely appropriate age for young women to begin exploring sexuality, but does not necessarily mean that they're ready to become sexually active. We are aware of flaunting our figure with more revealing clothing to look more sophisticated and sexier, but that is not an invitation for sex. Male or female, sex seems to be one of the top topics of conversation around that age and teenagers are all just trying to gain some insight into the taboo topic. From our first sexual experiences, young women especially confuse sex and intimacy. Sex is very different from the intentional act of loving and connecting with someone intimately. For women especially, sex and sexuality can become internalized as a source of validation, entangling our self-worth into how others perceive us.

Despite my shame and conflicted feelings in Scotland, I still wanted Craig's attention and grew jealous if he showed interest in the other girls. He reassured it was *me* and only me that captured his attention. I was special. We managed to conceal our stolen glances and flirtations from the rest of the group during the trip. The secrecy felt thrilling. My mind raced to thinking of the forbidden romances I had read about, especially since *Romeo and Juliet* was slated to be one of our productions the following school year and I was determined to be cast as Juliet. Craig made it clear to me that if anyone found out about our relationship, we would both be in serious trouble, but *only* because his older sister was my teacher.

When we returned home, Craig kept in touch through phone calls and we made plans to try to see each other. I worked at sneaking out of the house to see him, being picked up when my parents weren't home. Maintaining a secret relationship was starting to feel wrong, but I was easily reassured by simple gifts and his words that we were destined to be together. In addition to keeping constant contact with me by phone, he would find opportunities to come by the school theater when I had rehearsal, or drive by my home when he was at his college campus, less than a mile from where I lived.

Still into my twenties, I would ashamedly reinforce to myself that losing my virginity to him felt consensual. But looking back, all I can see now is the manipulation of an adult and all I can feel is heartache for a girl who never got the chance to wholly comprehend and agree to that major life transition. Predators seek the characteristics of the most vulnerable in the herd; the isolated and injured. I had very low self-esteem, few friends and was angry at my parents over the move to Missouri. My insecurity was desperate to be reassured and soothed, especially by a seemingly caring older guy. I liked the attention he gave me and everything felt more intense because it had to be completely secretive.

One night when he had taken me back to his sister's house while she was away for the weekend, he told me that it had to be kept secret because "my sister would lose her job." I continued reassuring myself that Craig was a good guy. *He's in college, he tells me I'm beautiful, and he even volunteers with the youth group at his church.* But something in my gut gnawed and left me on the verge of tears at times. I felt I was being pulled further away from my peers, as he would become jealous if he saw me being friendly towards any of the other guys in my drama group, so I began to avoid them. I was flattered when a senior boy in my theatre group asked me to be his homecoming date, but Craig was fuming. I reassured him that we would only go as friends, but I felt torn continuing to hide our relationship from everyone.

The large group of my drama friends that went to the dance together split at the end of the night, one home for a girls' sleepover and the boys at another. While the other girls laughed and gossiped together in the basement, I was upstairs alone taking persistent and supposedly urgent calls from Craig. He had called me several times wheezing, saying he needed to go to the emergency room, claiming the anxiety of me being at the dance and not checking in with him caused a severe asthma attack. I was starting to feel overwhelmed by Craig's demands and hurting my date through my seeming heartless attention that night.

Fed up with his persistence and emotional blackmail, I finally ended our interactions and Craig steered clear of me once I made it known I was no longer interested. The shame and disgust I felt from my own actions led me to hold on to this secret for nearly seven years, until I was the age he was when he had taken my virginity. For seven years that shame grew like a slow, drip-feed of poison, making me believe that I was somehow 'bad' rather than the victim. Grooming is a subtle art. It took years for me to understand the immense confusion that this situation created and that what happened to me wasn't my fault.

Working with women clients now, it is unfortunate how common this predatory theme has come up in our therapy sessions. Years later I would work with trafficking survivors providing equine psychotherapy and learned their experiences began the same way for them as well; a vulnerable, often under-age girl was targeted by an older guy who groomed her through a brief phase of acting to be her caring boyfriend. The cheap dates and gushy text messages were likely some of the first validation or forms of affection they had ever received. It is sickening that at the root of this exploitation, is just someone's young heart *desperate* to be loved, to be told that they matter or are beautiful. Even despite the extreme of trafficking, many women will quickly agree that how they lost their virginity impacted their belief of their own self-worth for many years.

More recently, I met with one woman in my office who was ashamed of an affair she had with her former college professor. Even 16 years later, it took months in therapy before she would stop matter-of-factly placing the blame and shame on herself. She had initially begun meeting with me to address depression and a prior eating disorder, but the affair was mentioned during a timeline activity meant to interpret how our major life events have shaped the way we currently view ourselves. It was no coincidence that her previous anorexia developed at that point in her life too, while her parents were distracted by the more destructive behavior of an older sibling. Not wanting to burden her parents, she became a perfectionist and even began taking college courses as a high school senior, where she met the professor. Finally, the disparity of power between her younger self and the college professor became clear to her.

"Do you know why the age of consent is 18?" I asked.

Her eyes looked up from where they had been resting in her lap, fighting back tears.

"It's because our brains are not fully developed until we are 21," I explained. "Our prefrontal cortex, the area responsible for judgment and critical thinking, is still not fully developed. We still have a child mind, and children make decisions on a need to feel loved and accepted. We often get sex confused with love and validation."

By this point the tears were streaming down her face. She, too, fought so hard to believe she had consented, but explaining it in this way broke the wall around her heart. She was finally free of the 'I am bad' belief that had infiltrated a marriage, a belief she maintained, reflected something deeply and innately wrong with her. She could finally grieve for the young woman who worked so hard to not be a disturbance, only to catch the eye of an older superior for his own gratification.

I continued to keep Craig a secret, but the buried trauma began leaking out as self-hatred, as I restricted calories at lunch at school and began superficially cutting myself in the privacy of home. My inner anguish and need-for-approval continued over the next few years of high school, when binge drinking and smoking weed on the weekends with my friends became the highlight of my week. At house parties, I acted out for attention and became heavily drunk. I recognize now that the side of myself I allowed to come exposed with alcohol; the sloppy, emotional and conflicted girl was really about purging the inner turmoil I was desperately working to conceal.

By 17, I felt that any remaining innocence had left me entirely. I began resenting anything associated with my younger self, including my poor horse Redwind. The simple joy I previously felt towards horses only brought more awareness to how tarnished and damaged I felt. I was no longer the sweet, wholesome horse girl. Rumors about me from weekend parties swirled throughout the halls of high school. Rather than fight to correct the stories, I leaned into the easier path of becoming who they assumed me to be. My heart hardened and so did the image I portrayed. I prioritized my popularity, theater and partying, while Red got pushed further and further from my heart and mind. My mom had luckily found a great boarding facility and I knew the next generation of horse girls there would be thrilled to have an amazing horse like Redwind. The owner of the barn knew of a family looking for a first horse for their granddaughter and I pulled the trigger on the sale. I just had to rip it off quickly and get it over with. I had one last trail ride with Red on a cold November afternoon. I knew not to allow myself to dwell emotionally on the finality of our relationship because I would fall apart. Maybe if I had sat long enough with the grief and guilt I was feeling, I might've realized I was turning away from anything that brought me genuine happiness. Instead of seeing my horse as the companion and friend who made my heart soar and grounded me with a sense of purpose, he had become an obligation I needed to remove from my schedule.

A year later and eager to leave St. Louis and my time in high school far behind, I had chosen a university in New York for a stark change in scenery. Without the familiarity of my social circle and activities of high school, I found myself alone in an unfamiliar setting and culture. Before I enrolled, I learned the school had an equestrian team and clung to the hope of joining to find some sense of identity at the university. In meeting the other girls on the team, I felt outside my element surrounded by young women who rode 'on the circuit', competing in hunter classes in the Hamptons. One girl even had her horse shipped to Florida in the winter, so she could continue riding. I couldn't even speak their language, let alone associate with this privileged horse world. There were other backyard barn riders like myself and another eventer from the West Coast, but my lack of knowledge of this larger horse world excluded me from the larger team. My weak riding skill became apparent in our twice-weekly lessons when I was paired with significantly better riders than myself. I started to drown again in not being good enough. I was drowning in no longer feeling validated by my peers from high school, struggling to make friends or feel a sense of belonging at my new college, my lacking performance in lessons and in classes, and my appearance. I continued lashing out at myself with a renewed self-hatred.

Self-harming is a behavior that typically begins in adolescence when teens try to externalize the internal conflict they feel. Simply, they want the pain on the outside to match the pain they feel inside. It's a negative coping skill that can escalate to become addictive and even dangerous, often spreading between friends as a learned coping mechanism. Without the skills to name and address their emotions, they send out a plea;

somebody please recognize that something is terribly wrong. While I hid the cutting on my hips and thighs, I became obsessed with making my physical size as small as possible. Maybe if it became severe enough, someone might notice.

The disordered eating I started in high school grew more prevalent in the first few months of college as I began restricting meals and purging after allowing myself even a well-balanced, healthy meal. When a roommate was in the room not allowing for the privacy of the toilet, I found the dingy, forgotten bathrooms throughout campus. My purse contained a bottle mixed with diet pills, laxatives and diuretics—all serving as a reassurance that I could eliminate a meal even if I couldn't find privacy in a bathroom stall. Alcohol and marijuana further helped to numb emotions while I used my performance with grades and riding competitions to gauge my own self-worth, usually punishing myself for any sense of mediocrity or disappointment.

Riding in New York felt incredibly foreign to me, not only in the culture of the other girls on the team, but in that I barely stepped foot inside a barn. Our horses were groomed and tacked, waiting upon our arrival. There were no stalls to pick, tack to clean, shavings to sweep, turnout schedules to be managed or jumping fences to be set up. I hardly knew the name of the horse I was riding at any given point and had no attachment to any of the lesson horses. Not only did I not feel a connection to the horse I was riding, I felt no connection to myself or my body. At shows, I focused on how I placed in each class for a sense of my value or validation. I wasn't ever interested in improving my riding, only to try to place higher the following week for a different colored ribbon. On the bus rides back to campus, I would sulk with my fourth-place ribbon, headphones in my ears, stewing in contempt for myself.

Now as an adult, I ache for that younger self, wishing I didn't spend all that time and energy directed at picking myself apart and hurting myself. I recognize the complicated emotions I was compulsively working to express and now look to serve as a positive intervention into a young person's life who may struggle with that same internalized anger.

The universe, in its mystical way, delivered such a girl to me as my very first client using horses in therapy. Taylor's father urgently scheduled a call with me after they had discovered copious small cuts extending the length of her forearm. Despite her parents' insistence, Taylor, then 13, clammed up and refused to discuss what compelled her to harm herself only protesting she hated everything about herself. Navigating their recent divorce, both parents were working at co-parenting the issue, torn between removing privileges, such as volunteering at the horse rescue I then worked at or finding a specialist to intervene. Like most adolescent clients, Taylor was guarded and dismissive during our first meeting. She offered little to no information on her inner turmoil. But her demeanor immediately shifted as we approached a certain horse she had grown fond of during her time volunteering. Now smiling as she stroked the stunning mare's face over the fence, I recognized some leverage to use the horse in our next session.

The following week I had the mustang tied and ready for Taylor to groom and asked why she was so drawn towards this particular horse. Brushing the mare's coat, Taylor noted her sweet nature and unique markings that made her stand out. It was clear Taylor also found a lightness or an innocence at the stables with the horses that was in contrast to what she was experiencing at school or at home.

Taking a bit of a risk, I asked Taylor to write each of the negative beliefs she held about herself on individual slips of paper. When she had finished, I handed her a small bag filled with clothespins and asked if she felt comfortable to read them out loud individually before clipping them into the horse's mane. She hesitated with a stunned reaction before pulling the first folded slip of paper out. *I am stupid.* Fumbling, she clipped it in the wavy black locks of the horse's mane. *I hate my nose. My body is disgusting*. For the first time I saw tears in Taylor's eyes as she added more insults on her beautiful horse.

Not wanting to cause further distress, I asked her to pause and tell me about her tears. With tears flowing down her cheeks, she choked out, "It's not fair to her, I would never say that to her."

"Of course you wouldn't, but you tell yourself these thoughts dozens of times each day," I offered softly.

Removing the clips from the horse, we went to sit down together in the shade of the barn. She admitted that a month prior, a group of boys had pulled her shorts down in gym class and laughed at her butt and underwear, which quickly spread throughout her grade. The teacher had been unaware of the incident and Taylor was too embarrassed to share the issue with either of her parents, feeling it was insignificant compared to the changes in their family structure that they were already dealing with. Taylor's story reiterates that no harming behavior emerges without a precipitating event. Like the pressure of a shaken soda bottle, trapped emotions can grow to be messy until we learn how to cope with them in small controlled ways. Using the compassion and love she extended to the rescue horse she admired, Taylor grew to reclaim a sense of compassion and empowerment towards herself and her body.

It wasn't until my sophomore year that I slowly started living more in congruence with my authentic self. A busier schedule with an increased course load left little time to ruminate in self-hatred and I had a great group of friends that year to return to. Feeling more connected to myself and my love for the outdoors, I considered transferring to a school in Colorado. I changed my major from nursing to psychology, feeling more invigorated by the new curriculum.

With my new course load and riding lessons filling my time, I suddenly had less time to focus on restricting food and managing a diet. I clearly remember stepping out of the shower one morning and glancing at myself in the mirror. I was shocked. I looked *great*. I looked healthy and lean, the body type I had been striving towards, but most importantly I was happy. By exercising multiple times each week and eating regularly, I had maintained a fit and healthy body without relying on any of the former harmful methods. Health was as simple as finding joy in an activity that nurtured my body and spirit, listening to my cravings and appetite, and beginning to believe that I was worthy of love and acceptance for the person I was. This realization came slowly in stages and at a time when I was ready to let go of all the ways I was harming myself.

During one of my riding lessons that fall, I was placed on a large, skittish warmblood for the first time and struggled to get him to enter the indoor arena. With his neck swaying back and forth, snorting at the dark threshold in front of him, I felt nervous and overpowered by the horse. The coach Sam, noticing our struggle, approached us and offered some advice, "Just remember that they're herd animals and looking at you to be the leader."

It was such a simple, but profound statement. I had never drawn any connection between a horse's innate nature and how we needed to use that knowledge to interact with them. Sure enough, as soon as I relaxed and made the mental determination that we would enter the indoor arena, the horse walked willingly forward. It was my first nudge from Equus, urging me to begin considering the larger perspective of how we interact with the environment around us. That moment also reinforced that my circumstances were contingent upon the mindset I held. Nothing else would change unless I was willing to believe in myself.

As we're developing throughout adolescence, we're processing feedback from our social interactions in the world around us to gain an understanding of who we are and how we measure up in the social hierarchy. The marketing industry is another type of predator that preys on our fears and insecurities, promising acceptance and status when we buy their product. Even long after we've severed ties, the false narratives instilled by a predator take time to detox from our system. We believe no one else will love us, that we are lucky to have their attention, or that we will end up alone, looking in from the outside without them. Slowly, we are worn down over time into a diminished version of ourselves. Stroke-by-stroke, stride-by-careful-stride, a predator makes calculated movements on our psyches. Often it is only through a hard awakening where we can be separated from the predator, and begin to address the shame, guilt or self-deprecating beliefs about ourselves that have become so ingrained into our thinking patterns. Our passions deflect and protect us from this negative outside influence, as we feel the discrepancies between a world where we thrive and feel seen, and a world where we are made to feel inferior, working constantly for validation that is always just beyond our reach. It is only in finding and clinging to something that gives us passion and purpose where the seeds of self-love and confidence are planted and nurtured again.

It takes confidence and assertiveness to defend oneself against a world that is always pushing back with whisperings of deficiencies and destruction. But after being continually inundated, our nervous system either is stimulated in hypervigilance or succumbs to a dissociated state. Either way, we are going through the motions of our days reacting to our circumstances, rather than fully living with mindfulness.

That nudge of confidence I felt leading the nervous horse into the riding arena made me feel capable again. I no longer felt stuck in the self-protective responses of fight, flight, freeze. Instead I felt that I was leading and directing my own life again. I needed to rediscover my identity, my true self, after years of struggling to fit in and follow the herd. And in that moment, I felt the shimmer of joy in being in congruence with something I loved again, more in alignment with my true character and heart.

4.

Pressure and Release

The excitement of living in proximity to the bright lights and buzz of New York City lost its luster after my freshman year and I started considering transferring universities. By my sophomore year, I had become more settled and made enormous strides forward in caring for my mind and body, living more in congruence with my more authentic self. As the cold days drew shorter and darker, my roommate Julia, who was also on the equestrian team, noticed I was still conflicted around changing schools. One night over dinner, she directly asked, "Well, where were you happiest?" I immediately recalled the feeling of riding Redwind out on the prairie, imagining the long grass with cottonwoods blowing their ethereal bolls on an early-summer evening. Her question unlocked the realization that nothing quite gave me the same satisfaction as feeling nestled against the Rocky Mountains underneath the vibrant cathedral skies. I suddenly felt a sense of relief deciding to return west and began applying to schools, working through the logistics of transferring.

Pressure and release is a negative reinforcement method commonly used in horse training of applying pressure and rewarding with release. Once I made the decision to transfer, the pressure that I had been putting on myself immediately began to lift. By the following spring, I was enrolled to begin my junior year at Colorado State University. Yet in those fleeting months of that winter in New York, I had begun dating someone. I had first seen Jason around campus and noticed he was a snowboarder and outdoorsman. Tall and muscular, his beard and casual dress was in contrast to the more preppy Lacoste-wearing aesthetic of the east coast culture around us. While a bit rough around the edges at times, I felt I had more in common with him as we were both enthralled by nature and outdoor recreation. When I mentioned that I was transferring, Jason was surprisingly also interested in moving to Colorado with me. Several of my friends voiced their concerns about the large commitment to one another so early in our relationship. My parents mirrored the same concern, too much too soon, but I was determined to transfer to Colorado whether or not he came along.

By August it was settled that the two of us were moving to Colorado together and we drove west with both of our cars full of our belongings. The return to Fort Collins for school felt like returning home, like the college experience I might have had if I'd never moved away from Colorado. It felt like a fresh start, that I could wash myself clean from the person who grew so destructive through self-harming, disordered eating and reckless behavior. I wanted to restore my image back to the open-hearted girl who loved the mountains. I knew she was still in there. I felt myself take a much-needed deep breath; finally close again to the mountains and my old community. Despite all this excitement, I was anchored to the commitment I made in moving into my first apartment with Jason, which would soon prove to be more difficult than I had expected.

I was naïve to what living with a partner would entail and bull-headed against the insistence of my family to reconsider and to live in the dorms for a year on my own. Jason and I were suddenly living two very different lifestyles, as he was not enrolled in school with me. It wasn't long before the differences in lifestyle and priorities slowly drove a wedge between us. I began to isolate myself more from seeking out new friends and attending social events on campus. We started arguing more and I saw a new side of his emotions that brought out the worst in me. By October, I realized we weren't happy or compatible. I felt embarrassed to have quickly confirmed my friends and parents' fears about living together. At the same time, I felt guilty that my parents had paid our deposit on the apartment, so I remained quiet, frozen in fear. I still encounter young clients who remain living in an unfulfilling or unhappy relationship out of guilt and minor financial obligation. I urge them that there is always a solution—your happiness and peace of being is worth so much more than an apartment deposit.

More than ten years later from my own experience first living with a partner, I would work with a woman who was battling her own depression and lacking relationship. Tabitha had first met Brian when she was 18 and had been waiting for nearly ten years for him to propose to her. Struggling with chronic health issues and depression, I first focused on building her self-confidence and pushing her to start engaging within her community. Building her social connections, she found a fulfilling job while studying full-time for a career in the medical field. We addressed previous trauma and mood swings related to her illnesses, but the more she described her home life, the more I wanted to focus on her relationship with Brian.

Over the first few months of working together, I noticed a pattern with Tabitha's mood and sleep that was influenced by arguments with Brian, where his hot temper could escalate into throwing things around their apartment and brutal name-calling. I pointed out how his behavior affected her and she agreed. She insisted he begin meeting with his own therapist, but she still had her heart set on marrying and starting a family with this man.

During one session, Tabitha wanted to address a binge-eating habit she developed in the evenings. She was ashamed by the behavior, which was in contrast to her strict diet that was fueled by health-related goals to help keep her physical symptoms to a minimum. She reluctantly admitted that she binged on junk food and would hide the wrappers from Brian, who would criticize her. As a therapist, I truly believe that each client is an expert of their own life. They recognize the same issues we see, but it's my job to help explore the resistance the client is facing from taking action to rectifying their situation. From my own experience, I know the decision to end a relationship is more impactful coming from the client themselves, rather than at the suggestion of a therapist, friend or family member.

Lost in the heavy feelings of tension and resignation, Jason and I drifted farther and farther apart. Outside of our relationship, my coursework and animals became my saving grace that semester, places of refuge and solace. That September at a local pet shelter, Jason and I picked out Riley, a black golden retriever and border collie mix and brought him home. Caring for a new dog helped to defuse the tension between us. It gave us a distraction as we took Riley on new adventures. Having a dog encouraged us to start exploring local trails, dog parks and meet our neighbors out walking their own dogs. We were able to develop more of a working friendship between ourselves and the arguments stopped.

Out of curiosity and boredom one night, I began scrolling through DreamHorse.com, looking at available horses in my area, when a chestnut Morgan gelding called Buster caught my eye. He was nearly identical to Red, even the star and stripe down his face and single sock on his hind leg were similar. The owner was seeking a 'care lease', meaning I'd only be responsible for the fees related to his monthly upkeep; his board, farrier and vet bills. Something about this feeling of returning home back to my childhood landscape and culture encouraged me to reach out to Katie, the owner, to see if leasing Buster could even be a possibility.

Katie lived down a long dirt road, north of Fort Collins against the foothills, raising a head of cattle with her husband. Buster had a background in English riding and jumping, but Katie was focused on raising young children and didn't have the time to continue riding him. After a brief ride on Buster in the arena, we finalized the lease agreement and I drove away eager with the anticipation of caring for a horse again. I missed the seemingly mundane routine of driving to the barn, picking stalls, riding and letting my horse graze after as a reward. Within several weeks, Katie hauled Buster in her trailer to the boarding facility I had found and lent me all her tack and equipment to start riding again.

I could feel my heart beating faster and fuller with each ride with Buster. Afterwards I picked his paddock in silence, when the heavy emotions I had been masking began to surface again. The simple pleasures in caring for Riley and Buster felt more rewarding to me than trying to connect with the larger social culture on campus. Being a transfer student made me feel like a bit of an outsider in addition to being stuck in a fading relationship. Sometimes feeling isolated, I felt myself growing more depressed again. Although in the few hours I visited the barn, I radiated with a new warmth and was held in the stillness around me. I also sought out an on-campus therapist for weekly sessions, but it was those quiet hours alone with Buster where most of my healing began to take place. On sunny days I would lay with him in the pasture while he grazed, and some mornings before class I would have the arena to myself, riding along with my music. I was still hesitant to truly share my emotions and let my guard down with my therapist, but riding and routinely connecting to Buster allowed me to express emotions without words in a setting where there were no repercussions or judgment.

As if compensating for the lack of control and hopelessness I felt at home, I buried myself in my schoolwork and maintaining a high GPA. Even though I had made enormous strides in caring for myself, the need for high achievement was still oriented on performance, but I loved my coursework on psychology and was easily motivated, hungry for more. I started working as a research assistant with several of my psychology professors and made new friends with other like-minded students who were also interested in pursuing an advanced degree. As most undergrads inevitably do, we became increasingly more quantified in our reasoning during these years—'if it can't be measured, it doesn't exist.'

Drawn to deducing something to its most minute form, I became interested in a potential career in cognitive neuroscience, wanting to measure neural pathways. "I would never go into counseling or working with people," I'd tell myself when the topic of grad school or careers came up.

In any introductory psychology class, one will inevitably learn about theorists Ivan Pavlov and B.F. Skinner. Their famed experiments with salivating dogs and rats pressing levers were the first studies on conditioning and learning. Dog owners know that their canine companions are more likely to repeat a behavior after being rewarded with praise or a treat—positive reinforcement. Horses are slightly more unique in that they learn from the release of pressure, or negative reinforcement. Negative does not imply punishment, but rather the pleasure associated from the removal of an aversive stimulus. A classic example is using pressure of a rider's feet and legs to urge the horse to move forward; when the horse complies, the rider relaxes their legs. In groundwork, pressure can be the use of body language; raising our shoulders or hands, walking towards a horse with intention. With precise timing, the softening of our movement and energy conveys to the horse, *"There*, that's exactly what I asked for." We reward horses with relaxation and peace. It's a misconception that having a horse continually repeat the exercise without a pause or acknowledgement of release would reinforce the learning. It actually only leads to confusion and frustration. Leaving the pressure on can create a lack of trust in their handler or trigger their need to flee. When people or animals are continually pressed without release, they either submit to learned helplessness or become angry and begin lashing out to find reprieve.

Jason and I couldn't be the partner that the other needed, but I knew ending the relationship would have to fall unto me. Jason had a difficult upbringing and feelings of abandonment were a recurring theme in his life, so he wouldn't separate on his own accord. I was stunned at the volatile behavior that could escape from us at night. Jason would throw open the car door while I was driving, threatening to jump out or I would break a lamp after swatting it off the side table as I retreated back into the bedroom. After the arguments began to escalate again that summer, I had rehearsed what the reality of a breakup would mean. Looking into Riley's soft brown eyes one afternoon, I'd play with the tuft of white hair on his chest, heartbroken knowing I'd have to leave him behind too. I knew I wouldn't be able to walk away from the relationship and take the dog as well. Jason had paid for Riley's adoption fee and was more entitled to owning him than I was.

A month before starting my senior year, I returned from my summer job and found Jason heavily drunk after spending the afternoon drinking with our neighbors. Feeling as if I was walking on eggshells, I attempted to make dinner for us, but became frustrated by his clumsy attempts at trying to help. "Here, if you just want to sit down, I can get everything ready," I insisted. I imagine he might have felt embarrassed for being drunk by late Sunday afternoon and only wanted to contribute, but it was easier for me to finish chopping the onion and simmering the meat in the skillet with more space in the kitchen. The tension continued to rise along with the pressing heat of our third-floor apartment that had little to no air conditioning.

We had been looking forward to an intentional meal together to work on finding quality time between us. So far, it wasn't off to a great start. I was irritated, hungry and feeling hopeless about salvaging any connection between us. I was envious of other couples our age that looked carefree and happy. Our relationship was so hard. Having just sat down at the table to eat, Jason immediately started talking about our troubled relationship. I told him it would be better to talk about it at a different time, but he doggedly persisted. With no release, I wanted it all to stop and covered my ears with my hands, trembling with frustration, shutting my eyes tight and willing for this to go away. I didn't know how to get us out of this situation and felt incredibly guilty for moving Jason away from his family and friends in New York, where he had a much better support system.

My mind was racing and I needed to find some space. Rising from the table, I tried to step around Jason to get out of the corner, where I felt overwhelmed and stuck.

"Where are you going?" he demanded.

"I… just need … to get out of here," I said, squeezing around the chair he was sitting in.

The last thing I saw was Riley cowering with his tail tucked between his legs when I felt Jason's hand grabbing my ankle and pulling me to the ground. Shocked by suddenly finding myself on the floor, I struggled to break free from under Jason's weight. I knew he wasn't trying to hurt me, but was acting out of a desperate plea for me not to flee and abandon him as so many people in his past had.

Somehow in the next few chaotic seconds, I stumbled up from the floor, grabbed my car keys and called for Riley to follow me. We raced down the flights of stairs and jumped into my jeep together. I drove away while Jason chased us, pulling at the door handles and pounding on the glass. I remember driving down the road to a nearby parking lot, my bare feet resting on the brake pedal. In taking some much-needed deep breaths, I began to process what had just happened. I knew for certain it was time to move out. The distress far outweighed the guilt of obligation to Jason, embarrassment and emotional attachment I had to our beloved dog. Riley was the final reason I had stayed connected to our relationship. I knew Riley would be well-cared-for by Jason, but separating from him broke my heart.

While ending a relationship feels difficult in the moment, hindsight always allows a change in perspective that we were insistent on making a square peg fit into a round hole. Jason and I were on two different paths and better things were to come for us as individuals. Jason also knew that moment between us had finally severed the remaining thread between us. He graciously helped me pack my belongings and insisted I could still visit or spend time with Riley when I needed it. Having a dog had been extremely beneficial for me that year, but I knew Jason needed the company of Riley more than I did. Several years later, the two of them would complete hiking the Appalachian Trail together and remained inseparable.

In many relationships, there becomes a moment where the tension of continuing to go through the motions becomes unbearable. Nearly after two years of therapy sessions, Tabitha finally recognized the constant pendulum swinging of commitment that she experienced from Brian and ended their relationship. She started reaching out to friends for support and reclaiming old hobbies. She realized how the unhappy relationship had isolated her further, only adding to her depression. Balancing the grief of losing her dreams of an impending marriage, she began to dream about how she would redecorate her space and spend the upcoming summer. As an artist, she was working to change her perspective to see the endless possibilities that existed on the blank canvas before her.

I was fortunate that in the same week I broke up with Jason, a spare room became available in my childhood friend Lauren's house near campus. I was released from the hypervigilance of living with the walking-on-eggshells feeling I'd endured for nearly a year. Living with other girls my age was the college experience I had hoped for. My evenings were replaced with wine nights and watching *The Bachelor,* and laughing with Lauren and our other roommate, also named Emily. I turned towards riding Buster and schoolwork with exuberance rather than desperation.

It was late fall of my senior year when several events would shift my neuroscience career focus into the profession I have today. One afternoon between classes, I got a panicked call from the stables. "Buster is colicking. I've already called the vet." My heart dropped to my stomach. I threw my phone and notebooks into my backpack before running down the steps of my statistics class. A worker from the barn had noticed Buster was exhibiting significant signs of colic, a sometimes fatal gastrointestinal condition that occurs in horses. I sped from campus through the streets of Fort Collins towards the barn, not sure what I would find waiting for me or how I would be able to help until the vet arrived.

Typically boisterous and aloof, Buster was ignoring the hay piled in front of him, his head hanging to his knees. Sliding past the door into his stall, I rested my hand on his shoulder and could hear his breathing wasn't right. "Hey bud, how are you doing?"

It wasn't long before the vet arrived and started checking his vitals, listening for gut sounds, and attempting to remove the blockage through intubation. Horses are physically unable to vomit, so if a horse eats something poisonous or has a food impaction, a tube will be fed through their nostril and down their throat, where water will be pumped in an attempt to stimulate a reflux. Every attempt had been made to alleviate Buster's impaction but he was declining quickly.

Defeatedly, the vet sighed, "He would need surgery at this point. It's expensive and I don't think Katie has that kind of money." The vet knew I was leasing Buster and wasn't responsible for making this decision, but calls to Katie from both of us had gone unanswered for hours. We had never addressed emergency procedures in our lease agreement and suddenly I was torn between putting Buster down or electing Katie to a roughly $10,000 surgery.

The vet gave us some time alone together in the stall, where I prayed with desperation, despite being a self-proclaimed atheist at the time, tears brimming my eyes. The horse that had typically ignored me and shown little-to-no affection draped his head over my shoulder and surrendered with a sigh. I could feel

89

the weight of his heavy head, the pain in his belly growing more uncomfortable and distressing by the minute. It was the first moment of Equus, that spiritual connection between horses and humans, that I had experienced in nearly two years. This time, I allowed my heart to fully feel it and savored the connection. Stroking his neck softly, I assured him he would be okay. I knew I couldn't allow him to suffer and was leaning towards telling the vet to euthanize Buster if we couldn't contact Katie soon.

Suddenly I heard the quick steps of the vet approaching. "Katie's on her way with the trailer," she called out. "She was out moving cattle with neighbors and didn't have cell reception."

"Thank God!" Blinking back tears, I couldn't have been more relieved. Less than 20 minutes later, Buster was loaded onto her trailer and headed into surgery. Weeks later, I was able to visit him after he had recovered and was resting back on Katie's land. That connection I experienced with him in the stall continued to linger. How can we measure a relational connection, especially with an animal? With my strictly analytic mind at the time, it seemed illogical that horses could be emotional or exhibit behavior beyond their natural instincts. Despite years of riding and spending time around horses, I knew they had plenty of intelligence but was still so naïve to their full potential. Horses are deeply complex and incredibly observant animals, but where they shine is emotional and social intelligence.

A dream I had several days later would further challenge the quantitative, strictly rational mindset I had developed through my studies. I dreamt of a field at the base of a large hill. Redwind, my first horse, was lying there in the grass and I understood that someone was with him and that it was time to say goodbye. It was a brief but powerful image. I woke crying out, tears streaming down my face. I had never woken from any nightmare or dream so distressed. In that moment, I felt Red was connecting to say goodbye, but I kept this feeling private, feeling a bit silly for thinking it could even be possible. Years later, I would confirm through my parents that Red had indeed been put down at that exact time of my life and have since heard similar accounts of other horse owners experiencing a horse saying goodbye at the time of their passing through a dream or a vision.

All within the same week, the Sandy Hook massacre occurred. Coming home after classes one afternoon, I saw aerial images of students and teachers being led single file out of a school by police on the television. My roommates and I watched in silence, sickened by the lack of compassion for human lives—children's lives. In the days that followed, I was stunned with the rest of a nation that was reeling in anger at a teenaged boy and politicians who pointed the blame at one another. As coverage of vigils began appearing in the news, I noticed a team of volunteers who brought in golden retrievers to comfort the victims and their families. If there was ever an epiphany moment in my life, this was it. I had volunteered at a therapeutic riding facility one summer during high school and was familiar with service animals, but this was the first time I had seen the validated use of animals in mental health treatment. Instantly, I knew my calling was to find a career connecting humans and animals and began applying to counseling programs. All within days of one another, these events beckoned me to consider the connective and spiritual nature of animals. That powerful connection I had experienced with animals throughout my life could be tied to my passion for psychology and I eagerly began learning as much as I could about this field. Seeing this new excitement in me, my family and friends began sending me newspaper and magazine articles of professionals in their area who were using animal-assisted therapy. I may have lacked the full courage of transferring back to Colorado on my own years prior, but the fire of applying to grad school with this career in mind made any transition or discomfort worth the risk.

Working with clients now, I reassure them that change only occurs from events that are difficult and uncomfortable. No one willingly makes a dramatic change in their life from circumstances that are pleasant or comfortable. The relationship that feels like a constant uphill battle, the job where we feel invisible or burnt out are all signaling us that change needs to happen. Change is scary and stressful. There will be added stressors associated with those decisions, the fear of disappointing people and, ultimately, the fear of the unknown. But there will come a time where the simmering pressure of not changing builds to become unbearable and we recognize that the uncertainty or fear of taking that next risky step will outweigh the distress of our current situation. And in time, after making that difficult decision, we will begin to experience that *release* of pressure; savoring the shift we have made, enjoying a higher quality of life and a newfound strength and resilience.

5.

Ask, Tell, Command

One of the most common aspects addressed in therapy sessions is learning when to take accountability for our own thoughts and actions, and when to consider how other factors may be influencing our situation as well. The environment around us, family dynamics or internalized beliefs, for example, each contribute to how we view and interact with the world around us. Until we are exposed to anything new or different, we are repeating the model we've been shown up until that point. Even working in the horse world, I still encounter great misunderstandings from horse owners when they fail to consider how diet, social stimulation or lack of environmental enrichment may be influencing their horse's temperament. Whether horse training, starting a family or a new career, we are operating on what we have been exposed to until someone suggests a different approach. Eight months after those moments inspired me to reflect on the connection I had always experienced with animals, I enrolled in Regis University's masters in counseling program. The shift from the funky, laid-back college town of Fort Collins to the larger city of Denver sometimes left me reeling as I navigated constant overstimulation of city life and a broader dating pool dynamic. Without the companionship of Buster or Riley, I wanted an opportunity to connect with animals and found an animal-assisted therapy program where I began volunteering.

Once a week I drove out from the central business district of Denver where I lived in my shared apartment to a suburb west of the city. I enjoyed the privacy of the backyard farm and house to myself in the mornings, caring for the horses, goats, cats, rabbits and rats that the program used in therapy sessions. I began to notice the horses there were a bit grumpy and ill-behaved. They weren't mindful or respectful like other horses I had previously worked with. Usually a bad-tempered horse reflects either discomfort or confusion at what is being asked of them by their handler and I could tell Cody, the chestnut gelding, was suffering from some type of pain or distress. One morning while navigating the feeder with my right hand, with two flakes of hay balanced on my left, Cody bit me in the back. Reeling around from the attack, I was stunned as a horse had never been aggressive towards me. A horse would typically never blindly attack a person, certainly not out of frustration from not being fed quickly enough. I felt the same reaction I felt when Jason pulled me to the ground over a year ago, the shock of him using his physical strength to intimidate me, my jaw hanging, eyes brimming with tears in betrayal. Feeling sad and upset, I left Cody's hay lying on the ground that morning and walked away across the frozen paddock to tend to the other animals.

The following week when I came for feeding, I entered the garage barn where the horses and goat's hay was stored and saw the entire shipment of donated hay was completely rotten. Repulsed by the browned and matted hay, I suddenly understood why Cody was so ill-tempered. His stomach was hurting and he likely had developed ulcers or other gastrointestinal issues. I made a note on the whiteboard to communicate the urgent issue to staff, but knew it probably wouldn't be addressed. If they couldn't recognize this moldy, rotten hay, which was not only inedible but harmful and toxic and could cause respiratory issues, it was apparent they didn't have the horse knowledge that I was interested in gaining.

Despite feeling disappointed with that first center, the experience helped clarify that I was only interested in using horses for therapy sessions. While I felt that interacting with all animals can be beneficial, I recognized that horses, being community-based prey animals, are most capable of reflecting one's emotions and the safety of the environment around them. For domesticated animals, horses are unique in this capacity and more likely to provide more genuine feedback to their handlers or those seeking insight into their own emotions and behaviors while interacting with them.

A few months later, I found a working student position at a riding facility in Littleton, exchanging barn chores for riding lessons. Several hours each week, I would manage the turnout schedules of horses stabled in the barn when they would get their daily time in the dirt paddocks to stretch and roam, hand-walk injured horses in the soft indoor arena footing, clean tack and grooming tools, all while basking in the presence of roughly two dozen horses. I was finally relearning barn management skills and observing horse behavior with a new lens. There were numerous horses that exhibited anxiety in different ways, 'stereotyped behavior', as they are collectively referred to when an animal displays repetitive movement. Much like a big cat in a zoo enclosure, some horses will restlessly pace back and forth behind the bars of their stall or paddock.

One horse, deemed too dangerous to be handled, would weave or sway back and forth on his front legs, using the momentum of his large neck, indicating distress and self-stimulation. Deacon was a large bay warmblood with a previous career in jumping. Little was known about his background, but the beauty hidden behind the pinned ears and curled nostrils caught my attention.

After a few more months passed, I couldn't ignore Deacon any longer in between my chores and began approaching him through his stall door when no one was around. The other staff members had warned me that he lashed out through violent biting. Still determined to show some compassion for this animal, I would halter and tie him in the stall, so that I was safely able to groom him and he grudgingly allowed me to, ears pinned back flat. But as the new grass of spring began pushing its way from the thawed ground, I was able to lead him outside and hand-graze him around the property. With the brief encounters and routine, I watched a misunderstood and angry animal soften with simple pleasures from the new attention and stimulation. Problematic animals are often ignored or neglected, as untangling their behavior takes time and patience. Shutting an anxious, large horse into a stall with little room to move or interact with other horses definitely wasn't helping his behavior and he grew louder in protest. The now-calmer horse was soon relocated a few weeks later to be a 'lawn ornament' for a family that had plenty of pasture where he could graze, never to be confined to a box stall again.

In my counseling classes, I was beginning to feel more like the horse girl from childhood, as every major assignment started to integrate an equine-assisted psychotherapy approach. As I progressed further into the program, I began to be recognized by colleagues and professors for my interest in incorporating horses into counseling.

In addition to studying counseling curriculum, I discovered an organization that provided education and accreditation for becoming a therapeutic riding instructor. Teaching would create a more stable stream of income since I had been relying on gig work, everything from writing assignments and promotional events to dog-sitting and nannying. I found a therapeutic riding center near Boulder that was willing to supervise candidates in training for the certification process, which included collecting supervised hours and several exams. I emailed Betty, the head instructor with Rocky Mountain Riding Therapy, and organized meeting that weekend.

Pulling up to the small community stables, with the Boulder Flatiron mountains rising dramatically from the plains like the jagged shoulder blades of a prowling mountain lion in the background, I started feeling anxious whether I could meet the requirements of this year-long commitment.

Soon after meeting Betty, I began volunteering in their riding lessons, either leading the horse or walking alongside the riding participant while they rode, if they required additional physical support or balance. The riding instructors at RMRT reflected a deeper, more spiritual connection to the horses, which may have been in part due to our proximity to Boulder, but I appreciated the nurturing community they had created. They considered the preferences of the horses; what types of lessons or activities they excelled in and, more importantly, which they showed a lack of interest or disdain for. Much like people, horses thrive in jobs they enjoy but can become restless or irritable in ones they do not, leading to behavior that escalates and can be dangerous if left ignored.

Starting my second year of grad school, I was feeling encouraged professionally and more grounded overall living in Denver. Wanting to add a companion into my life, I began searching for the golden retriever I had always wanted. One cold, rainy afternoon in October, I met a woman I had found online in a parking lot who had advertised two golden retriever males left in the litter that her two dogs most recently had. Cautiously, I told myself that I was only there to look, not wanting to commit to the first puppy I interacted with. From the back of her van, the woman pulled out a large plastic container with two joyful, pudgy puppies and my heart clenched at first sight. Squatting down to greet them, the smaller of the two immediately reached out to lick me. I was instantly hooked by his outgoing and friendly temperament. In an instant, his big-eyed gaze and unbridled joy melted my resistance and I knew I couldn't leave without him.

The exchange became slightly uncomfortable when she asked that I pay in cash. I would soon learn this tactic of meeting in public with no papers was entirely indicative of puppy-mill behavior. If I had listened to that gut feeling, perhaps I would've recognized the discrepancies, but I was enamored by the wriggling, doe-eyed puppy in my arms. Driving home, I smelled the scruff of his neck and warm belly smell of new puppies, and soon the squirrely puppy fell asleep on my lap. "Aw, you're all tuckered out," I cooed to him. And that's how Tucker came to be in my life.

Throughout the days, I balanced working on assignments and studying for my riding instructor exam while trying to tire out the enthusiastic puppy. At the time I was sharing a condo with a roommate and our building had a communal backyard where the other neighbors let their dogs and puppies play, creating a bigger sense of community where we grilled together on weekends or relied on one another for help with the dogs. As Tucker grew larger and more coordinated, I took him hiking on weekends and to different parks and patios around Denver, loving having a constant companion by my side.

Having passed the requirements for the riding instructor certification, I began teaching two group lessons on Saturdays with participants of varying levels of verbal ability, physical muscle tone and comprehension. One of the students, Billy, a 40-something man, had been riding with RMRT for many years and was there for engagement and fine motor tasks. While non-verbal, I quickly noticed he was much more perceptive and intelligent than he was initially willing to share. After gently mounting his horse, a volunteer would lead him around and he would close his eyes, lifting his hands in a gesture that was not too dissimilar from the meditative stance a Buddhist monk might use. Our goals were encouraging him in horsemanship to hold the reins, follow verbal prompts, such as reaching for objects planted in the arena as he rode, and encouraging him to open his eyes and connect with us. Walking alongside Billy listening to the rhythm of the horse's gait, I would often glance up to catch him peeking at me out of the corner of his eye before he quickly snapped his eyes shut and tilted his head away again. If we could motivate him to hold onto the saddle horn for balance, we would encourage the horse to trot for several strides. Jogging alongside him for additional safety, I'd look up to catch a glimpse of his smiling face, which sometimes couldn't contain his joyful laughter.

Working with this population gave me huge empathy to the parents and families of those with differing abilities. I would watch the caregivers nap, read a book or scroll through their phones for the hour of their child's lesson. Exhausted from the constant care and attention they provided, they seemed grateful for a moment's rest. I loved feeling like I was serving a purpose in someone's week, building our relationship together over the weeks and months. Despite physically taxing work and coordination, I felt proud in my growing professional identity.

With Tucker nearing his first birthday, I was entering the final year of my graduate program but was still looking for an organization to shadow that provided equine psychotherapy. I found Pikes Peak Therapeutic Riding Center and contacted their program director Jody. I drove down to Colorado Springs to meet her one afternoon and was captivated by her spirited heart and red curly hair. Jody explained that she would be supervising my co-facilitation of a group with a woman who was working towards her licensure as a therapist. Once a week during my final fall semester, I would rise before dawn to begin the two-and-a-half-hour drive from Denver down to Colorado Springs. Despite the dark and quiet city streets, I felt an energy pulsing through me as I navigated through the narrow roads and onto the highway. Typically with that timing, I'd see the looming crest of Pikes Peak about an hour into my drive, just as the sunrise illuminated the plains and purple mountains before me.

The groups I was helping to co-facilitate and observe were structured around a 28-day drug-and-alcohol rehabilitation center for adults. Rita, the therapist and other facilitator, would greet myself and two other volunteers in the morning, assign horses and set expectations for the two-hour session. With such high turnover within the population of our groups, we typically cycled through three lesson plans: one where we would give an introduction to horse behavior and grooming; another where members would be partnered together and working on leading and setting boundaries; and a final challenge where partners would have to lead a horse through an obstacle course together. The high turnover also gave me the chance to meet so many people and see potential epiphany moments the horses offered weekly. While every individual may not have been an animal lover, I imagined each participant was at least grateful for the equine sessions for a change of scenery from the residential facility in which they were staying. The warmth of the sunshine, expansive skies and feeling of being nestled on the lap of the mountains all created a healing environment, and most people can find some semblance of peace within that setting.

I remember one incredibly brief interaction with a woman after we had introduced the concepts of how horses show emotion and preferences through their body language. She was standing to the side, a bit disengaged. I could tell her head was circling back to another time and another place. She shared with me that she was a former racehorse trainer and jockey. "I didn't know *any* of that," she whispered, nodding towards the horses, almost in tears.

I, too, remembered the immense guilt I had felt once I began to recognize how incredibly sensitive and empathetic these animals were. The professional horse world can still resonate with the mentality that they are stupid animals meant to be dominated into performance for the sole purpose of the pleasure of the rider. Holding emotional space for the moment, I stood beside this woman and wondered how the same mentality of that world had inevitably victimized her as well.

It was during my time co-facilitating these groups where I learned my absolute favorite intervention for equine-assisted psychotherapy: 'ask, tell, command.' This simple exercise illustrates the use of healthy boundaries and confrontation while also introducing the method of pressure and release, which is how horses learn new skills and communicate with one another. Standing at the end of the lead rope in front of the horse, the participant is tasked with getting the horse to take a step backwards, using only body language and the rope to communicate.

Kim, one of the long-term volunteers, would demonstrate the concept and skill for the group by using the analogy of a parent asking their child to brush their teeth before bed: "First, they're going to *ask* you, but say you ignore them; the second time, they're going to approach you with a firmer tone, "Go brush your teeth." Now, if they have to ask you a final time, they're going to use your full name and ensure you hurry along to go do it." This would usually get at least a smirk from the participants, understanding the concept of applying more pressure to guarantee a result. We all respond better to being communicated with using the softest voice of 'ask', but we also can't keep asking someone to do something or respond to us, if we're being ignored. Ask, tell, command helps to instill a set plan of giving two opportunities before there is firmer intention to guarantee a result. This exercise also inevitably reveals how someone approaches confrontation.

Kim would then demonstrate the steps of ask, tell, command standing directly in front of the horse. First, the person will lean forward and look the horse in the eye to communicate intention and to seek the horse's attention. The 'ask' is simply waving the index finger back and forth of the hand not holding the lead rope, which typically will not produce a response unless the horse is extremely familiar with the exercise and the participant conveys strong intention. This is always a good opportunity to enforce the idea that we can 'ask' someone repeatedly, wearing ourselves out, and still not get the desired response. Our 'tell' is now waving the lead rope with the other hand while also continuing to wave the index finger back and forth. The pressure of the lead rope swinging now creates an irritating factor on the horse's face and some horses will back away at this step. However, when a participant is new to the exercise, they will almost always have to go to the 'command' level, which is taking a step towards the horse with intention while waving the lead role with one hand and their index finger with the other. Approaching the horse with this level of conviction can feel threatening or provoking to many people, and I can watch their body language crumble the second they begin to move towards the horse. If they don't get the horse to move back, they will almost always laugh and say something like, "I don't want to be mean!"

Equine therapists believe that there's much to be learned by observing how different people react or interact with horses. Those with emotional wounds can become whittled down in time, lead to believe they are asking 'too much' from others, that they would be disappointed with the outcome anyway and choose to retreat inward. It can feel uncomfortable to take up space, to speak up. I typically have a conversation with most of my clients on their relationship with confrontation and work to separate it from the idea of it conveying a fight, argument, disturbance or provocation. This is especially true for young women in a culture that has generally praised them for being agreeable and compliant. When working with horses, these individuals need to learn to become comfortable asserting themselves at times when it can become a safety issue. A horse with poor physical boundaries can be as dangerous as a partner with poor relational boundaries.

My dream of doing equine psychotherapy while still in its infancy was growing more tangible each day. I could feel my shoulders drop emotionally, growing more confident in myself and my abilities. In my dating life, however, I was growing more discouraged. After a handful of hopeful relationships that would suddenly turn cold after a month or two, I was working to be more intentional and selective in my dating. At the bequest of a counseling supervisor, I learned about attachment styles and identified negative self-beliefs with my counselor in my own psychotherapy sessions. Journaling one evening, I narrowed my priorities in a partner down to three major ones: he has to be outdoorsy, love animals (or at least tolerate my obsession with them) and have a career that benefits others.

As summer lost its glint and shifted into fall, I met William, a tall, handsome young medical resident with a crown of faded copper hair above sparkly sea-blue eyes and an inviting smile, through a dating website. I was immediately charmed by his southern accent and easygoing nature. We could talk about everything and nothing; MLB standings, our favorite books, asking playful theoretical questions that revealed values and parts of ourselves that had been buried deep. He was an incredible fly fisherman and skier; well exceeding my outdoorsy quality expectation.

After several weeks of dinner dates, we were planning ski trips together and camping adventures for the following summer. As for wanting to marry someone who had a career that impacted others, he was training to be a cardiothoracic surgeon at a teaching hospital in Denver. He was remarkably intelligent but down-to-earth, and I was smitten. Even Tucker would be rigid with delight and anticipation of the dependable roughhouse playing with William when he walked through the door. There was just one problem. Three months into our relationship, William invited me to the National Western Rodeo with his work associates. It felt like a big step in commitment to be meeting his colleagues. Having grown up going to the stock show and rodeo in Denver, I was excited to share this tradition with someone I cared about. While I don't attend too many rodeos, they are undeniably a huge piece of western culture and I appreciate all forms of equestrian sport. The stock show takes place in Denver each January and is a local tradition celebrating how animals and humans have collectively shaped the culture and landscape in settling of the American West. While the crowds may be a bit boisterous and the events a little jarring, I also love any opportunity to throw on denim, boots and a felt hat.

Halfway into the bulldogging, or steer wrestling event, William looked restless sitting beside me and asked if we could step outside. I followed him out of the arena and through the doors leading out on the street, confused by the sudden change. After a momentary pause, my heart thumping in my chest, he broke the silence, "I have to tell you something… I'm allergic to cattle."

Relieved, I could feel the ten-pound weight leave my chest. I laughed and said, "Cattle?"

"And horses."

My smile quickly faded. *Who was allergic to horses?* "Like hay? Most people are allergic to hay or dust or—"

"No, like horses. I almost died once on a tail ride when I was a kid."

I staggered, my mind racing. What did this mean for us? I had never expected to find a partner who rode or shared my passion for horses, so was this even a big deal? Then he said that he needed to leave the rodeo from feeling an oncoming allergic reaction, so we awkwardly said goodbye to the group before leaving.

As we walked across the sprawling parking lot to his car, the uneasy silence between us was unnerving, my mind trying to process the information. *"Wait,"* I said, turning to face him. "You still like Tucker, right?"

I needed a partner who supported my passion for horses, but I didn't need them to be involved with my work or hobby. I was sure we could navigate this without issue. But my dog? Well, that would've been a deal-breaker.

Despite his allergy, I was filled with momentum and confidence, progressing more seriously in my relationship with William. Now at the finality of my program, I was entering the internship portion where I would begin seeing clients and running wellness groups for a large community health organization while still working as a therapeutic riding instructor on the weekends. I'd sometimes question whether William was as supportive or engaged as much as I would've liked him to be, but reasoned his demanding workload and studying took most of his time, so I was grateful to receive the remainder of his attention and free time.

In August of 2016, I graduated with my degree in counseling and made my first attempt at starting a private practice. Knowing nothing about business, I registered my LLC and found two different horse therapy nonprofits that were willing to take me on as an independent contractor. Starting my career and living on my own for the first time, I felt emboldened and excited for this next chapter. At one of the facilities, I met supportive friends Mary Ellen and Mallory, who were also my age and both pursuing careers in equine-assisted psychotherapy. We navigated the logistical aspects of starting private practices together while sharing the same passion to share our wisdom of horses with others.

I was thrilled to have the independence to begin creating lesson plans and interventions for clients and actually working in the role I had dreamed of over the past three years. But the hours spent commuting and long days prepping and running back-to-back lessons took a toll on me mentally and physically. Sometimes I would teach up to ten adaptive lessons each day, in which I averaged walking a mile for each lesson, following the horse on the uneven arena footing in various temperatures and weather. If we didn't have the necessary number of volunteers for a lesson, I would have to fill in as a side-walker, while simultaneously teaching a lesson and directing volunteers. Factoring in the additional two hours of commuting and walking Tucker before and after work, I would crawl into bed some nights nearly in tears from exhaustion.

The momentum into my dream career lasted a few months before the reality of making enough income to support myself became more pressing. Even though I had the support from volunteers, the other therapists and instructors, as well as the parents of my participants, I continually felt pulled around by the founders of the organizations I was working for. They were both asking more of me, more of my time, time creating new programs, running groups, volunteering with fundraisers, coordinating with other organizations—all with the promise of much-needed and deserved compensation in the future. Initially I complied for a while.

By November, reaching desperation to support myself, I resigned from one of the horse facilities and began working as a clinician providing wellness courses at a community mental-health organization. The disorganization and lack of transparency with finances I had already encountered in the nonprofit world left me feeling defeated. I began to question whether a career in equine-assisted psychotherapy was even plausible or what I had envisioned it to be. I felt disheartened that, despite my years of studying and volunteering, the reality of doing the work I intended seemed like a fantasy. There were few opportunities where horse facilities were open or compatible for a mental health provider and I needed the stability of consistent income. I meditated and prayed for help in this decision process. Sometime

114

during this time, I wrote my desired salary of $60,000—far above what an unlicensed therapist like myself could make at the time—on a piece of paper and continued to look at other careers and deliberate with family and friends.

Starting in the classroom during childhood, girls are taught to be polite, quiet and compliant, whereas boys are reprimanded for their wild and unruly behavior. Girls are subconsciously internalizing which behaviors are more socially appropriate based on how they are being praised or rewarded. However, they don't teach us that those rules do a 180-degree turn entering into the workforce and those same young women struggle with feeling invisible and overlooked. We still believe that if we keep our head down and do our work that someone will take notice and we will be praised with accolades and promotions. But the unruly men are the ones getting those accolades and promotions because they *ask* for it. They raise their hands in meetings, interject, volunteer for new projects, and that is how superiors take note. No one told us that we would have to learn to be uncomfortable stepping in, asking for what we need and setting expectations; things by our very nature that seem pushy and demanding. That doesn't imply that you need to become a corporate shark, you just need to learn to stand your ground.

It can be a slow process for women to unlearn the misconception that we should not take up space, that asking for, or rather telling someone our expectations, would be considered abrasive and rude. But seeing this concept in action with a horse, it made complete sense. We need to raise the volume deliberately to reach the desired response as quickly and efficiently as possible. This is never done in anger or in an attempt to control, but a mutual understanding that I expect the horse to respect me as much as I respect them. The beautiful thing is once we start feeling comfortable with taking up space, sharing ideas, setting boundaries with others, our self-confidence and self-esteem inevitably rises along with it.

The ask, tell, command activity helps us to embody that grounded energy and debunk the myth that others will "be mad at me" when we ask for something we need to feel even secure or valued. I was willing to jump through hoops and take on extra responsibilities through those positions in the hope that the founders of the organizations that I worked for would take notice and reward me with more compensation. Instead, I was strung along with empty promises, much like the ones I had heard from the romantic interests in my early twenties. I determinedly wanted the title of being an equine-assisted therapist or someone's girlfriend and clung to whatever promises I was given like a life raft, rather than communicate deliberately what I needed. While I felt justified in my resignation from the horse-rescue facility knowing I had more potential and seeing no forward opportunities, I still felt ashamed and embarrassed that I wasn't able to pull off my dream. I was still hoping for a miracle.

6.

Join Up

There is a beautiful technique in natural horsemanship called join-up, which occurs in a circular enclosure known as a round pen. The intention behind the activity focuses on communicating with the horse without using speech or touch, but instead through body language and directing one's energy appropriately. The process starts by using pressure to drive a horse away from you, which asserts your leadership, and then inviting the horse to come back and submit willingly to you. Without the pressure of whips, ropes or equipment of any kind, the horse will follow the handler, glued to their side despite changes of direction and pace of walking. It is the first concept in 'gentling' a horse to begin accepting a saddle and later, a rider, on their back. In introducing this activity to clients, I always start with a question, "Have you ever heard the term *breaking* a horse, or someone referring to a horse as being *broke*?" Many will nod or acknowledge that it refers to a horse being trained. "Well, the term comes from how we used to train horses many years ago, which was pretty brutal. Horses would be tied to a post, usually having their head or legs

119

tied in uncomfortable positions, and the horse would fight the constraint for days without food or water until they surrendered. They *broke* the horse's spirit."

By this time, many clients become quiet or uncomfortable. I can usually recognize the ones who have experienced physical violence themselves. They know too well what a broken spirit feels like. I would continue by telling a story: "There's a famous horse trainer, who grew up watching horses being 'trained' this way by his father, who was also physically abusive to him and his brother. When he was finally old enough to leave home, he moved out to Nevada for work and began observing the wild horse herds in the Sierra Nevada Mountains. He noticed how when a young horse misbehaved, the momma horses would push the baby away from the safety of the herd, essentially sending it to its room. Being away from the safety of the herd is especially frightening because the baby horse is now more vulnerable to predators. Recognizing the need for the safety of the herd, the juvenile horse will begin showing submissive signs by lowering their head and licking and chewing with their mouth. They are acknowledging they will comply with the structure and rules of the herd members, if they will be allowed back in. Using the same concept, we can now gentle horses in a very peaceful way."

In the round pen, I'll demonstrate how we 'send the horse away' using our body language with the addition of either a lead rope or a flag. With the horse trotting around in a circle, I will instruct the clients to look for the inner ear to become fixated on my voice, the horse's head turned in towards me and not outward, the lowering of their head, and finally, licking and chewing with their mouth. When I see those signs, I relax and turn my back to the horse, signaling they can approach me. With our predator-prey dynamic with horses, our eyes pointed at a horse can imply pressure and intention that can direct a horse's movement or send them away. When the horse is several feet away, I will softly raise a hand back towards them, an invitation to connect. The moment when the horse accepts this invitation by extending its nose out towards the back of my hand is the purest form of joy I've ever experienced, and it's the same intensity each time that I feel it. I see that same feeling on the faces of my clients as they experience that connection for the first time as well.

The horse will stand, licking and chewing, a submissive and relaxation response, as I softly stroke their neck and shoulder emphasizing the peace experienced from working in compliance with my leadership. The final test for determining whether the horse is fully in congruence with your energy is when you take several steps forward and the horse follows behind in step, with a nonchalant demeanor, entirely relaxed. I will demonstrate that the horse should follow if I turn right, or back left, if I speed up my pace or slow down to my 'old lady walk.' I joke that I want horses my entire life, and that even when I'm hunched over and shuffling my feet, a horse should be gentle and match my pace. It's not too dissimilar from having a dance partner.

It is the same feeling we strive for in our work and our relationships, that congruence with our fate. It is neither good nor bad, just a wholehearted acceptance for what it is. And as such, it is perfect. Throughout my life, I have frequently lived against the congruence of what is typically best for me: comparing my body to others; fixating on hoping to meet impossible standards; and morphing myself to better suit the needs of someone else's perception or idea. But I have been fortunate enough to have the wisdom to listen when the sound of hoof beats enters my story again. Horses are where I am grounded, my most authentic self. The times when I have been open and congruent to receiving their lessons, I have had numerous doors open and connections that continue leading me back into my work.

I can remember walking across the pitch-black parking lot to my car one evening after a long day of teaching at the ranch, still feeling discouraged with myself and hopeful for an opportunity to continue working with horses. I felt my phone vibrating in my bag and saw it was from Rita, the therapist I shadowed at Pikes Peak Therapeutic Riding Center the previous year.

"Emily, I just had the greatest chance encounter with a woman I met at church," she said breathlessly and explained how she had noticed someone new several weeks ago standing alone, so she had approached the woman to introduce herself. "We got to talking and she asked what I did for a living, so I explained. And she told me that her husband has an equine-therapy program and they're wanting to expand into Colorado!" I could hear the excitement building in her voice. "The facility they're needing a therapist for is in Evergreen. So I recommended you."

Words were stuck in my throat, feeling so appreciative that Rita had felt I was worth referring for an incredible position.

"Now Emily, this is a big deal. This comes with a salary of $60,000."

My feet stuck to the pavement and the duffle bag full of riding gear I had been carrying to my car dropped to the ground. I was speechless as Rita continued to explain the program and how they would contact me.

"Rita," I managed to squeak out, "I've been praying." My throat muscles were tightening as I tried to hold back tears. I explained how defeated I had been feeling about my job prospects lately, looking at different career paths even, but had been focusing on that specific salary as a goal to meet my needs. I could hear Rita becoming emotional too. It wasn't necessarily about the income. I took its serendipity as a sign that I was to continue my path with equine-assisted psychotherapy, now with this non-profit organization called Mustard Seed Ranch.

Brothers Tom and Ken had founded the program in Southern California ten years prior, when their faith and success in business called them to find ways to contribute back to their community. They were eventually drawn to the vulnerable youth in foster care, wanting to offer a sense of visibility and support. The two men had used their network of friends and associates to fund programs at stables where, at no cost to the participants, groups of teens would meet with a team of mentors who would instruct them in basic horsemanship skills as it paired with a larger lesson that would aid in processing their past emotions and encourage their potential. Mustard Seed Ranch was well-developed with author and psychologist Dr. John Townsend helping to create the curriculum that entailed setting boundaries, expressing grief, establishing trust and safety, and healthy communication, among other topics.

As their vision and organization expanded, they networked with other philanthropic individuals who were willing to act as benefactors for more programs throughout the country. This model in seeking individual benefactors helped stabilize the financial stress that most nonprofits experience. With a guaranteed salary, the time staff previously spent on fundraising and managing several roles could be directed to the sole purpose of providing services to the intended population. Having recently experienced feelings of hopelessness and burnout from working within nonprofits, it almost seemed too good to be true.

Rita had also recommended our supervisor Jody from Pikes Peak Therapeutic Riding Center for the role supervising the Colorado programs and I was thrilled at the potential to work under her guidance. After my initial interview, I remained in contact with Tom, the co-founder, but was eager for a response as it seemed like such an incredible opportunity. I felt myself growing anxious and frustrated when weeks would go by with no communication or if an additional task was added to assess my qualifications, as if they weren't fully convinced yet.

Much to my relief, I was thrilled when they eventually offered me the position, but was slightly disappointed when aspects of the agreement were adjusted. They justified that I was young and inexperienced, only adding to my determination to show my value and commitment to this new role. Jody helped to reassure me by reinforcing my capability, "Just remember that you have *way* more experience in this field than they do." She urged me to remain patient and not to become intimidated by their brusque, business-like manner. Overall, the men were supportive. I had a stable income and private facilities in the foothills outside of Denver and was working with my favorite mentor. I had so much to be grateful for. I reviewed the materials they sent and wondered how I would navigate a role as a leader in a faith-based organization. While Tom and Ken envisioned Mustard Seed to be more of a ministry-based service, I was a mental health professional first. While at its core Mustard Seed was a religious organization, its goal was never to convert children to Christianity, but rather to help them feel God's love for them and know that they were valuable. I reasoned that through my role, creating a safe environment for healing and using the horses and mentors, we could help them to feel God's love without needing it to be overt.

In order to grow the Mustard Seed Ranch location in Evergreen, my next steps were to begin contacting community partners to introduce our services to see if they were willing to send ongoing groups of participants to the ranch for programming. Many were skeptical about a faith-based organization offering free mental health services, but equine therapies were becoming increasingly popular and most organizations couldn't afford the additional cost of sending participants to an additional therapy. The California programs worked specifically within foster-care populations, but we expanded our requirements to include any adolescent who had experienced abuse, neglect or trauma. I was able to establish working relationships with three main organizations who came for weekly sessions. The participants of any given group rotated depending on who was currently enrolled at their facilities.

Now with the opportunity to live closer to the mountains, I moved from the heart of Denver out to the foothills of Golden that spring. My new home was near the ranch in Evergreen and conveniently located between my boyfriend William and my friends who lived downtown. The slower-paced lifestyle of living in a smaller town with an unbroken horizon suited me much better. No longer inundated with the constant stimulation of living in a city, I took what felt like the deepest breath in years. I was feeling confident in my new role at Mustard Seed, reassured of my path, but seemingly overnight, my relationship with William began to crumble. We had been together for a year and a half, but I felt I was slightly more invested in our relationship that he was.

One of my first major responsibilities for Mustard Seed was planning a barbeque inviting our community partners to the ranch. Tom and Ken were flying in for the event and our benefactors were attending as well. Using this as a great opportunity to showcase my capability, I worked on planning the event for weeks. When William forgot about the barbeque, I was crestfallen. I felt him continue to grow more distant, but whenever I questioned whether anything was on his mind, he denied anything was bothering him. His cryptic communication left me waiting by the phone, my entire headspace fixated on what was happening between us, a feeling that I dreaded. I associated it with all the worst qualities of myself, the overthinking, insecure rumination that pulled any focus away from any other aspect of my life.

Despite the desire for whatever rift had been thrown between us to vanish, with a single text conversation, the rug was about to be ripped out from under me. Within a week of the distance growing like tension between us, an old roommate of mine had texted me: *Hey, are you and William still dating?* She was out in Denver with friends that night and saw him with another woman. It was like the air had been punched out of me simultaneously as my stomach dropped to the floor. In the days that followed, I reeled from the betrayal, while also feeling so stupid for ignoring that feeling in my gut that had been working to warn me. After confronting him, I learned that William had been talking to this woman for weeks and had explicitly told her that he was single. How could I ever trust somebody's reassurances to soothe my growing fears or anxieties again? I would replay the weeks leading up to the incident, looking for any sign of trouble or where something had it gone wrong. The budding confidence I had just begun feeling vanished, leaving me feeling insecure, with the 'I'm not good enough' narrative repeated like a broken record in my head.

Like sending a horse away from you during join-up, creating separation is where the true growth occurs. I used the heartache to reflect on my direction in life, the characteristics of a partner I was hoping to find and, crucially, reinvested time pursuing opportunities and activities that I didn't prioritize while I was in the relationship. Putting the pieces of a relationship back together is not always a possibility, but putting the pieces of yourself back together after a breakup is a necessary yet painful chore.

It was ultimately the horses and ranch of Mustard Seed that became my saving grace and refuge that summer. On my way to the ranch each day, I could feel my spirits climb along with my car as Tucker and I drove into the spruce-studded foothills that grew more dramatic with each passing minute. Turning into the dusty driveway, my heavy heart was thrilled to be greeted by the small herd of ranch dogs, while the horses grazed together on the hillside. I spent many warm afternoons lying in the pasture, as the herd grazed around me, while the Colorado sun filled me with its warmth. What warmed my heart was when the plodding hooves and dropped noses of curious and concerned horses who would approach me. The initial blow of air that horses use to explore tentatively would wait for my hand lifting in reassurance before their jaws would resume chewing and they would return back to grazing.

Free in this setting I would pray, meditate, play and write: *Lying in the soft bed of pine needles, where I imagine the hooves of elk stirring to make their own resting place each evening, I disappear between the crisscrossing of strands to observe the clouds pass overhead. Rolling to my side to tiny worlds of pinecones, beetles, wildflowers and crumbling rocks, I retreat to this place to mend the brokenness. When I feel utterly alone in the world, I find my way home here to be embraced.*

It felt like a cruel twist of fate. Just as I begun to settle into the contentedness of attaining my dream job, I was reeling from a broken heart. Hiking out into the pasture before or between my group sessions, I could ground myself in the beautiful surroundings, listening to the wind whistle through the pines and long pasture grasses and allow myself the privacy to tear up and feel hurt. Occasionally the call of a red-winged blackbird from the cattails around the pond or a red-tailed hawk circling above would break the stillness. From the slanted hillside of the pasture, I could look out across the barn and arenas, the wooden fence line stretching like sutures across the land.

Anyone who's spent time around animals knows the magical feeling of when another creature acknowledges the emotional pain they sense from us. A curious horse would prick its ears at full attention, watching me find a place to sit and then snort and shake its mane, marching over to understand why I would place myself in such a vulnerable situation. You see, to a prey animal, sitting or lying down makes one vulnerable to predators in that they are no longer able to quickly flee if there was a threat. A horse herd has an orchestrated system to allow one or two horses to lay down at once, while the others stand watch. Horses sleep standing, but they can only enter the precious REM sleep cycle that allows dreaming when they're lying down. This accounts for why horse owners become concerned if a horse refuses to stand—it is clearly ill or injured enough to negate their highly-instinctual safety drive.

Humans have an instinctual drive that is not too dissimilar. If a person becomes physically ill, we know to remove ourselves from the village, family or community to keep the others healthy. With emotional illness, we still have that reaction wanting to isolate ourselves from others, without fully understanding why. Those moments where a horse would nudge me with its velvety nose, as if asking if I was okay, was enough to spread a smile across my face to know the pain I was feeling transcended the species barrier. There are situations that can't be fixed, where words are useless. Sometimes all we need is for someone to sit beside us in our pain.

It was around this time, as Mustard Seed was still in its infancy, that we had one such boy in one of our first groups who was very much wanting to isolate from all others. His mother had passed away fairly recently and his father was unable to cope with the heartache of losing his wife while simultaneously raising a child who was also experiencing their own grief. The sadness was thick and palpable in the air around him. From the long, dark hair that covered his face, the hunched posture and slowness of his movements anyone could look at him and see the illness—the hurt that he was feeling. A wisp of a boy, Levi was quick to be pushed from the center of the group in the excitement and energy of the other boisterous teens.

I remember looking for an opportunity to reward him with a 'special snack', a reward I created where if one of the participants would go above and beyond in their skill or participation for the week, they could request a food of their choosing for the group to share the following week. When you live in a residential treatment facility, you have no choice over your circumstances, daily routine or even what you eat; simply anticipating a food you've been craving can help motivate you through the week. I wanted Levi to feel seen and orchestrated a task for him to succeed in to be 'selected' for the special snack. He chose pizza for the group and mentioned he and his family always ate black olives on theirs. The pizzas were ordered and an extra can of sliced black olives were on standby to make certain the details were perfect. I remember watching his face bite into that cheesy pizza. It wasn't the same, but I could still see the momentary bliss of returning to those memories of eating pizza in peace with a family intact. Sometimes food can be the magic that brings a family member back, even for just a second.

While pizza can certainly be a miracle worker, Levi didn't move past his grief with that one meal. Over the weeks, he became more attached to Shiner, our small cutting horse. Slight and diminutive himself, Levi was a good match for this horse. The problem was, as a previously very well-trained performance horse, Shiner was still sensitive to leg and seat cues. While great in experienced hands, highly sensitive horses are not a good match for beginners, who are likely to be subconsciously cuing their horses unknowingly through being slightly off-balance in their seat or squeezing their legs in nervousness. I wanted the pair to work as did the volunteers, who also noticed Levi's interest and enthusiasm growing week by week working with Shiner on the ground. In the saddle, we spent extra time working with Levi on slowing his horse down when he broke into a trot and being mindful of relaxing the tension in his legs and body when he became nervous.

As weeks turned into months, the group progressed to light trotting, where I would allow them to trot down the long side of the arena, and bring their horses back to a walk on the short sides. Levi and Shiner became alive during the trotting. It was almost as if he needed the adrenaline of a moving horse to remind himself that he was still alive and present, that he could still experience happiness and joy, even if briefly at first.

The following week the boys assembled inside the door eager to hear the lesson I had planned for the day. There was a new boy with a soft and beautiful face standing near the back. Keeping him in the corner of my eye, I started to address the group on checking in on our "peak and valley," or the high and low point from each boy's week, and then plan for our activity that day. One of the counselors spoke up, "Did you see Levi cut his hair?"

Stunned, I stared into the face of the soft, beautiful boy standing in the back that I hadn't previously recognized without the long, dark hair. Embarrassed with words frozen in my mouth, all I could manage was a smile. I didn't recognize Levi at all. With the curtain of long hair gone, I stared at the face of a vulnerable child, who was bravely willing to re-enter from his dark night of the soul. Not wanting to bring too much attention to him, I smiled, complimented him on his new haircut and continued the check-in.

Later one of the staff approached me, trying to hide her smile. "Levi asked to get his hair cut so that he could see better when he rode his horse."

Tears sprung in my eyes as words continued to escape me. "I can't believe it."

"We gave up asking him months ago, but the other night he just came up to me and asked to get it cut before today. Before he rode." Pausing, I could see her eyes misting too. "I said, 'Sweetie, I'd be delighted to make that appointment for you.'"

Grief can feel as if the darkness just came up and swallowed you whole; that the pain will never go away. I like to remind clients at that moment that everything is temporary. No matter how terrible the feeling, how bad the situation, it is temporary and it will pass. Someday you will find yourself laughing at a joke when you thought you could never be happy again. You will find yourself smiling and admiring the beauty of the mountains, when the world once felt so cruel and unforgiving.

And maybe when trotting on the back of a horse, you will hear your heart beating, *I'm still here. I'm still here.*

7.

Prayer Flags

When we started the equine therapy programming for Mustard Seed in Colorado, there were three main organizations willing to shuttle several groups of their teenage residents to the ranch for our weekly sessions. The circumstances around each facility varied significantly, but they filled our mission of serving fragile hearts, lashing out and desperate for comfort and reassurance. I never asked for a diagnosis or background of the clients, as they were already receiving individual and group psychotherapy. I only emphasized that anyone was welcome to participate as long as they were safe to transport to the ranch that day. We didn't want our program to become a reward for good behavior throughout the week. Those that were hurting or acting out were the teenagers we especially wanted to come work with us and the horses. Because we didn't know their diagnoses, there was no preconceived judgment of the individuals participating or their past, each week was an opportunity for a fresh start.

Working as a therapist, we are invited into the most vulnerable and fragile aspects of a client's journey and inner psyche. It is such a privilege to walk alongside someone in these moments, often learning more about an individual than many of those in their closest circle. Despite the depth of these connections, we learn to say goodbye, most often never hearing from our clients again. The teens who rotated through my year at Mustard Seed were no strangers to transitions and goodbyes themselves. Those in foster care changed homes as frequently as every several months, while the longest residential treatments lasted one to two years. One of the tenets in creating any psychotherapy group is establishing a termination session that addresses the foreseeable change to the group and the acknowledgement of the completion of our time together.

Having first seen the colorful cloth strands hanging around doorways and patios in small mountain towns as a child, I was drawn to the beauty and mysteriousness of Tibetan prayer flags. As a sacred Himalayan tradition, prayers written on blue, white, red, green and yellow cloth squares are strung between trees, boulders or doorways. The colors represent the five natural elements of the earth, each flag stamped with the woodblock-printed image of a horseman and a prayer. The strung flags are offered as blessings meant to be carried by the wind for the benefit of all humanity. With this in mind, I created the practice of making and hanging prayer flags in the pasture for each group as they finished their time at Mustard Seed Ranch. Given many of our participants had little permanence to cling to as something that was theirs, I wanted to develop the tradition of a ceremony recognizing their time together, as well as to create a physical mark they could leave at the ranch. I dreamt of a stand of pine trees growing more and more colorful with the addition of more flags, reflecting each participant and the impact we had made.

From their first moment here, I emphasized to each group that while they shared the ranch with others, for the few hours they were there each week it was truly theirs. Our time together may have been very limited, but I wanted each teen to feel the consistency in caring for 'their' horse each week, knowing Tucker, a blur of gold fur and long limbs, would come bounding to greet them every time in the parking lot, and that there were adults who wanted to hear about their week with no ulterior motive. How much we can take for granted until we have stepped into lives where parents, whether consistent or capable, or homes that were secure and peaceful, would be considered absolute treasures.

While the traditional prayer flags display the woodblock-printed prayer and horseman, I asked each participant to write their own stories and messages on our cloth flags. For each of the five colors, participants were asked to write and reflect on the five questions, starting with: *What is something I am willing to leave behind or forgive?*

Transition allows us to take inventory within ourselves and reassess what we're carrying with us and whether it will be necessary moving forward. For many of us, there is pain and hurt emotions that cling to us, yet holding on to resentment and anger is like drinking poison and expecting the other person to get sick. The adolescents at Mustard Seed had every reason to be angry and hurt at the unfairness and injustice they each experienced daily and the loss of a secure upbringing, and angry at adults who were meant to protect them and had failed. Although anger and fear can be helpful in protecting us in the short-term, it begins to close us off from new people and experiences if left unresolved.

And then, *What is something I am looking forward to?* and *What is something I wish for myself?*

I also wanted them to hold hope for their futures. Sharing their hopes and dreams in a tight-knit group put them out into the world, making them real. By simply speaking their dreams out loud, I hoped they would sit like seeds, that time and nurturance could guide those dreams into fruition. I knew those who had aged out of foster care or who were already on probation had a much steeper climb ahead of them, but I wanted that flame inside them that dreamed of something different for themselves to continue to be stoked. The greatest gift we can give one another is hope.

And then, *What is something I wish for others?*

In wishing for something in our own lives, we have to reflect on whether we are willing to return that same offer back on to others. Despite being angry at a world that can sometimes seem against us, we must never lose sight of holding empathy for those who have wronged us, strangers we fleetingly interact with and the 'otherness' of those we may disagree with.

And finally, *What have I learned from being at Mustard Seed Ranch?*

Sharing as a group with chairs circled in the arena, each member would read their responses on their flags aloud while one or two horses roamed at liberty in the arena around us. We would then tie the strands of colored cloth to baling twine, our own construction of the prayer flags, and hang them with the others in a stand of pine trees in the pasture. There was always a palpable excitement as we all walked out of the arena and up the hillside, with Tucker happily padding alongside us, to add that strand to the growing collection in the trees; how sacred for an individual to hang their dreams and prayers among so many others. The breeze would whistle through the pine needles, sending the flags fluttering in the wind like the wings of birds. The volunteers and

I always looked forward to the day we would do the prayer flag activity with a group.

We hoped to hear that our time and our mission with the horses had somehow made an impact, no matter how small, into some of these lives. Hearts were typically opened and closed-off teenagers shared beautiful sentiments:

I have learned to enjoy the little things in life and worry about myself. Also, I have gained confidence.

I'm taking delight away from Mustard Seed Ranch.

I have learned pride and patience. Also, I have discovered the feeling of sharing a connection with someone even after a short period of time.

For some kids who had never expressed pride in themselves or felt a safe community of adults supporting them, it was a simple gesture that hopefully held deep ripples as we sent them back out into the world. Goodbyes are difficult for everyone. But transitions can be especially difficult for someone who has gone through the up-and-down uncertainties of the foster care system. I loved that the prayer flag activity was for the entire group, where we could all acknowledge the bittersweet feelings of parting, while recognizing that the brief connection made can last a lifetime.

Late that summer, while sitting under those prayer flags, I would meditate and reflect on my time with Mustard Seed and my relationship with William. Two months after the shock of the betrayal had ended our relationship, I received an email from him asking to meet. After months of working to stay distracted to prevent the recurring thoughts of different narratives racing through my head, the thought of closure was admittedly tempting. I believe we have all weighed the risks of offering a second chance to someone or to a partner who has caused us emotional pain. No relationship is free of challenges and strain, it is difficult to know where to draw boundaries and where to extend forgiveness. In his final year of medical training, William was now expressing his intention to a life-long relationship with me. Hesitantly, I reasoned only time could tell whether he stood behind his words and whether my trust would ever recover.

Choosing to commit to our relationship again, I also had to consider the reality of an inevitable relocation to his home state of Arkansas, where he had already accepted a position with a surgery group. I was excited for this next chapter with its many promises but also fearful of the uncertainties around whether we could mend our relationship. My feelings and opinions wavered back and forth, like a sewing needle. I daydreamed about southern living, yet it was no secret to anyone that my heart was breaking at the thought of leaving Colorado again. Coming home to Colorado and, ultimately, myself had been such a lengthy journey. I was worried about losing myself and my happiness by putting my trust back into someone who had recently broken it. I was also proud of myself where I had landed professionally. Running Mustard Seed Ranch was an absolute dream for me.

With Tucker exploring the pasture nearby, I pinched the loose, silty soil between my thumb and pointer finger and placed it in my mouth, swallowing it as best as I could. Like some primal instinct, I needed to feel that it would always be with me; the minerals of the soil would by some process become enmeshed with the minerals of my bones.

What do I wish for myself? I wished for what so many women wish for, to have a home and a family with someone I loved. That dream had seemed so close, just within my grasp before the infidelity. When relationships end, we also have to grieve the fantasy of our futures together—trips planned, collective dreams shared, the lifestyle we imagined are lost too. I knew deep down that I was still clinging to the hope that the dream wasn't lost, that it could somehow be resuscitated.

What was I looking forward to? The previous few months strengthened assurance in myself professionally, as I had built a successful program with nearly a couple dozen participants weekly, and personally, knowing I deserved more out of a romantic partner and could confidently ask for it. There was inevitable risk in both choices, but I was willing to try for something new rather than live with regret of not having tried.

What was I willing to leave behind or forgive? I wished that I could leave behind the betrayal of loss of trust, but I accepted our relationship would always be different moving forward, better or worse. I wished I wasn't so apprehensive about moving out of state; could I willingly leave again? Colorado was associated with the happiest years of my life, but maybe I was chasing the past rather than a place.

I associated the empowerment from no longer carrying the weight of our pasts with one of our groups, a court-mandated program for girls who had experienced the sleazy world of sex trafficking. The men associated with that world are incredibly intimidating, threatening violence towards the girls or their families, leaving them paralyzed with fear from seeking help or pursuing legal action. Even more disheartening, the men who seek the companionship of children can hide behind the façade of helpers in our society; respectable professionals, politicians, law enforcement or clergy. While unfortunately prosecuting minors for prostitution is still practiced in nearly half of the states, in Colorado these girls had typically been charged with drug possession or other misdemeanors and given the option to attend a program like theirs as part of their probation. I was excited to form a partnership with the organization, but also undeniably apprehensive on how to approach these young women. They were victims of horrific abuse, but I knew not to underestimate their internal strength and resilience. I didn't want to be viewed as another know-it-all adult in their world, but wanted our time together to be intentional and taken seriously. After a few initially slightly standoffish weeks together, one of the staff members, whom I later learned had been trafficked herself as a teenager, began to reach out and offer some guidance. One day in particular, she had warned me that one of the participants was in an especially irritable mood, after the girl had been denied permission to attend her former high school prom due to her behavior.

"They just want to feel normal," the mentor reminded me. It was that simple. All that they were craving was a sense of normalcy or familiarity in their world. They were tired of adults treating them as victims, as criminals or as ruined young women with poor judgment. They were under enormous pressure each day to meet the requirements of parole and school, an endless list of rules and adults watching their every move. We are so much more than the worst thing we have ever done, but sadly these girls were still carrying the shame and repercussions of their past. After that conversation, I shifted from the structured activities I typically used and tried to be more relaxed in allowing them some freedom in how they wanted to spend their time at the ranch. Some days we just groomed the horses and braided their manes. Sure enough, they started opening up more about their social lives and experiences.

When you are actively working to change your life or circumstance, it can be counterproductive to be continually reminded of your past. The girls were living examples of what a gift the freedom from our past can mean and what a relief we can experience when we are no longer burdened by its weight.

What did I learn from or take away from Mustard Seed Ranch? Mustard Seed was an incredibly special place, where I was reassured of my capabilities in myself and learned to remain faithful that everything will turn out okay, even if sometimes the path doesn't necessarily take the direction you envisioned. I learned much more from each story that a participant was willing to share with us while we worked with the horses. The change of perspective from hearing so many different backgrounds humbles us, providing some clarity around our own grievances and disappointments.

Milton Center, another major organization we worked with, was a well-known facility in Denver that housed difficult-to-place teenagers who were either removed from their homes or awaiting placement into foster care. In my site visit at Milton Center, I was initially impressed by the facilities, which were fairly new and well-maintained. Inside I caught glimpses of the reality of those children's circumstances that broke my heart. I met with their director as she led me on a tour of the main building, walking past one child who was having an emotional breakdown in the hallway and being comforted by staff as their cries reverberated down the hall. Artwork hung on one wall and I approached to admire it more closely. One drawing showed the scrawl of a younger child who had drawn smiling stick figures with lopsided hair standing in front of a home, underneath the words: *My wish is for a family and home.*

Shame boiled over inside me, as I reflected on how my own grief over the loss of a relationship had recently affected me and how it paled in comparison to the grief of a child who simply wished for the structure and support many of us take for granted every single day. Rebounding quickly to join the director who waited for me, we left to admire the gym and classrooms. Outside the main building were a series of 'cabins' where the kids had their rooms, grouped by gender and age. The smaller buildings were much older and, looking into the rooms, my shame only grew. The residents were allowed very few personal items and the rooms were bleaker than any college dorm I had ever seen. The only personal items or self-expression allowed were black-and-white printer pages that the kids had found online of different athletic logos or images they enjoyed. I had even taken for granted the freedom and resources I had to express my personality and interests my entire life; my friends and family even *celebrated* them. After the tour, I walked back across the parking lot to my car. Once inside, I buried my face in my hands and sobbed. What a great reminder that the misery of my own circumstances at any given time would be many children's fantasy life.

What did I wish for others? I wished that others could find the feeling of being loved, starting with friends and animals to the larger community and world around them. I wanted them to feel hopeful in the solitude of nature and the horses, like the younger child that was able to explore and feel free. I wanted their hearts to open again; knowing that in their pain they would also feel joy again soon and that everything is temporary. I wanted them to know that there were good people in the world, who had no hidden agenda, other than to see them succeed in

149

growing their self-confidence and reclaiming interest in life again. And I wanted the larger community to remember that we are all interconnected, that we need to take care of one another, especially the natural world around us.

With all of our participants, part of our weekly two-hour group sessions involved spending the last 30 minutes debriefing together about our experiences with the horses that day over snacks. It was essentially a bribe on my part: we're going to talk about feelings and emotions, but I have granola bars and fruit snacks.

It became interesting watching how each group acted around this time. The more traumatized group from Milton Center, kids who had undergone a *lack* mentality, still felt resources were scarce and would immediately shove one or two snacks into their hoodies or pockets before selecting the one they wanted to open in front of the group. This is the same mentality that causes hoarders to fill their homes and have difficulty throwing away or parting with possessions. Living with scarcity that directly threatens your basic needs or sense of security is a difficult knee-jerk reaction to undo.

There were also subtle individual reactions I wasn't always aware of until the director of Forest Heights, the residential facility for boys, called me and said, "We have to talk about the snacks." My stomach dropped hearing him over the phone, certain I had caused issues back at the residence due to my naivety. "You have some peanut-butter crackers right?"

"Um, yes," I started, "but I—"

"Keep buying them."

Still hearing my heartbeat thrumming in my ears at the fear of potential ramifications, he continued, "I don't know how much you know about James' background, but he is seeing us partially due to anorexia. Most days we can't get him to eat anything, but we noticed he eats two of those peanut-butter cracker snacks every time he's at the ranch."

I was stunned by this news. From the outside, James looked like many pubescent boys who shot up like a bean pole overnight while the rest of their body hadn't caught up. I also hadn't realized that Forest Heights had a standing practice that peanut butter was not allowed on site to prevent any upset, should a kid with a peanut allergy become enrolled at any given time. Without knowing, I had provided the forbidden treat to these boys.

Grateful that I hadn't caused any issues, I assured the director that we would always have plenty available. Without knowing his diagnosis, I had also allowed James the freedom and discretion to eat a snack in peace like the rest of his peers. I know many others who have come through my practice have expressed the conflicting feelings that arise when parents or peers know they are struggling with a mental health issue. They suddenly feel under a microscope. Emotional pain is largely invisible to others and can be extremely challenging for a child or adolescent to identify or communicate to parents or other adults. Self-harming can result as a way to physically manifest the internal wounds that feel difficult to describe or attempt to alert others for help. While some of us might struggle to empathize with eating disorders or self-harming, we all know the feeling of suffering alone, feeling invisible or feeling helpless.

To someone who is struggling with disordered eating, the thought of food itself or eating in front of others can be distressing. Maybe it was the exertion of hiking around the property, or safety of not having attention drawn towards him, but we can never underestimate the power that a simple action of trying to make others feel welcome and comfortable can have on someone's life. With such contrasting socioeconomic differences between the two groups, providing snacks meant so much more to each for very different reasons. To the kids at Milton Center, 'I see you, I appreciate you being here and there will always be enough.' And to James, 'I see you, I see your pain. You no longer have to hurt yourself to feel seen.'

The teens of Mustard Seed embodied the struggle of ambiguity in transitions, of letting go while also looking ahead. Their stories could be summarized in the renewed hope of a blossoming life free from the labels of a diagnosis, or being identified by their traumas. I offered to wipe the slate clean for the youth who came to Mustard Seed Ranch every day, yet I struggled with it personally in my own life.

As fall slowed into the winter months, I was still struggling on a decision with the future of my relationship with William. I found myself at a fork in the road, with one path leading to comfort and familiarity of my life in Colorado and the other leading to what I imagined was a bright and loving future with William that brought risks. I was conflicted about moving to another state for him, leaving behind family, friends and a job that I loved to preserve our relationship. I spent long, agonizing hours talking to my friends about the uncertainly of uprooting myself and re-establishing my life someplace new. My gut was telling me conflicting things, but I reassured myself that many couples make compromises and trade-offs in order to stay together. While we wish the world could be divided evenly— black and white, right and wrong—life is not separated by fairness or by order. A relationship will always skew one direction and with each new situation, we can't help but to consider the past as we anticipate the future. Much like the duality of the prayer flags, we can acknowledge the polarities throughout life, while struggling to find our place somewhere in the middle.

I wished for a hopeful future for every individual who participated at Mustard Seed Ranch, much as I wished for a hopeful resolution for myself.

8.

Engage, Disengage

In every encounter working with a horse, we are always extending an invitation that the horse can accept or decline. Reading a horse's lack of interest or ambivalence in the moment is an opportunity to reflect on and adjust our own expectations, but requires humility and patience in our fast-paced world. There are two sides to every relationship, two stories to take accountability for. With a horse we can only guess at what may be affecting their mood, and that's assuming we are even willing to listen. It can be as subtle as changes in weather, an upset stomach, a new horse added to the barn changing the herd dynamics or a sensed tension or anxiety from us. What matters is our recognition that something is off and a willingness to address the issue. Ignoring a horse's pinned ears or swishing tail to continue with our ride will inevitably escalate the resistant behavior.

Much like in our human relationships, poor communication leads to poor outcomes, often leaving both sides feeling emotionally exhausted and frustrated. William and I had been working to resolve broken trust to give our relationship

155

another chance, but there were fears and uncertainties that both of us were holding on to. There is always an inevitable risk in the unknown, but taking chances is how we grow. Horses take a risk each time that we halter them and lead them out of their stalls. They don't know what will be asked of them, where they will go, whether they will come back. Our demeanor in that first interaction with them is where they assess whether the risk feels justified. I felt I was willing to take that risk in my relationship with William, as he had been showing up, day after day, putting in the effort to reassure that decision. After months of feeling on the edge around any special occasion, he asked me to marry him and I accepted.

We celebrated our engagement and the finality of his arduous medical training with friends and my family in Colorado before William was off to Arkansas. I put in my formal resignation to Mustard Seed and to begin transitioning out of my responsibilities for the next month. In early September, with bittersweet goodbyes behind me and our belongings packed, Tucker and I headed east, with the morning sun rising over the eastern plains, eager to walk through the front door of our new home in just 12 hours. Saying goodbye to the ranch, the mountains, my family and friends had been heart-wrenching, but equally I was hopeful and excited about this next stage of life.

Having just reached my own professional goal of providing equine psychotherapy services, I wanted to continue with that momentum. Fortunately, I had found a therapeutic riding facility in Arkansas that provided both adaptive riding and mental health services. Nestled in the Ozarks, Equestrian Bridges was founded by a woman of my own heart. Shanna kept the organization going in its infancy by taking out credit cards, stubbornly impassioned to keep it afloat. After securing consistent funding and programming for Equestrian Bridges, Shanna had been looking at expanding into more mental health services for a larger community impact. It felt serendipitous to find another flourishing program in my new community. Having my own outlet to continue working with horses, I felt more encouraged by the potential in my decision to move for William's career opportunity. Once I had been settled for a few days, I was to meet Shanna and view the facilities where they kept their horses and ran programming.

I turned down the gravel driveway flanked by white wood fencing, the boards covered in a mossy residue adding to the white barn's southern charm. When I stepped out of my car, I was immediately hit by the humidity, something I was still trying to acclimate to. Luckily, there was a hint of a bite in the September air and I was relieved to have missed the brunt of the summer heat.

David, a slightly intimidating older gentleman with a white beard, flannel shirt and black felt hat, greeted me in the office and introduced himself as the equine manager for Equestrian Bridges. With his own background in natural horsemanship training, he had been volunteering with the organization for several years since his retirement. After quickly sizing me up, David led me to the indoor arena. Spinning on his heel to face me, he pulled a plastic container out of his back pocket, pinching something inside before stuffing it into his lower lip, all without breaking eye contact with me or missing a beat in his questions about myself, which were starting to feel more like an interrogation. *Was he putting chewing tobacco in his mouth?* I tried not to react, but was so unaccustomed to the practice. William 'dipped' in extreme secrecy—something I learned over a year into our dating, but he was still the first person I ever knew to use chewing tobacco.

His voice now slightly muffled, David told me to halter one of their horses to lead into the arena. I knew then that my real interview process had begun. I hadn't expected to be horse handling that day and remember feeling slightly annoyed. My nerves were still a bit fried from the long drive and unpacking. David pushed me to demonstrate ground exercises I had little familiarity with, all while quickly pointing out every time my hand held the rope incorrectly or my timing was off by a second. With my frustration growing, I masked it with a thin smile.

Two hours later, I thanked David for his time before leaving the barn, feeling fragile and discouraged. My annoyance brimmed around my eyes as I drove back out the driveway. The reality of integrating into a new program sent my emotions into a minor tailspin. I didn't want to have to start over with a new program, with new expectations and standards of protocols on horse handling. I had loved Mustard Seed and still believed it to be the absolute peak of my short career. I felt it was only too cruel to finally reach that landmark before having to choose between it and my relationship. The transition of leaving our lives in Colorado was still painfully fresh, and my optimism for marriage and starting a life with William could quickly flip into sadness and discouragement that it wasn't taking place in Colorado instead.

An encouraging phone call with a friend that evening soothed my worries. After a good night's sleep, I was feeling more determined and reassured. I continued to show up at the charming weathered white barn with green trim several days each week for horsemanship lessons with David and to observe current programming, so that I could soon begin teaching lessons and taking clients. The rest of my time I spent nesting into our new home, planning for our wedding set for the following fall in Colorado and exploring my new surroundings.

When William had first asked what he could offer to help with my transition, I was honest, "I just need to be able to ride." Horses would always be the grounding element for me, no matter what environment I found myself in. Despite the new and unfamiliar southern life around me, I knew finding a barn community would be that foundation where I could build my own community in Arkansas.

I found a local riding facility to start taking jumping lessons and enjoyed having the discipline of preparing for a lesson each week; grateful for an hour or two where I could disconnect from my anxieties and worries. The large warmblood gelding that I took lessons on was incredibly capable and gracious with his patience with me as a student. Simultaneously, I was starting to incorporate the more advanced horsemanship concepts that David was teaching me in between the adaptive riding lessons I started teaching at Equestrian Bridges. No element of the interaction with his horses was rushed or overlooked. In addition to grooming the horses before their lessons, they were always stretched and led through a series of ground exercises meant to assess their physical and mental capacities at that moment. If any horse showed any sign of discomfort or deviation from their usual temperament, they were pulled from their lessons from the day without a second thought. My favorite new skill was the concept of 'engaging' certain parts of a horse's body for movement and flow, using the subtleties of body language and cues. These were concepts I was also working on with my riding lessons, engaging a horse's hind end, for example, leads to compulsion of forward movement. This engagement and, conversely, disengagement in both riding and groundwork, were more advanced components where the handler was directing the horse's body for more intentional movement. One that was more difficult, but overall more conducive for better form and movement. These are the intricate elements where the hobby of horsemanship becomes an art form.

I had felt confident in my riding, knowledge of behaviors and handling, but pairing my riding lessons with groundwork started to feel like a new level of mastery. I recognized I still had a lifetime of learning ahead of me with horses, but only felt excitement with the new curriculum and world I was introduced to. I became a huge advocate for the importance of horsemanship skills and groundwork, David's philosophy echoing in my ears: "If you can do it on the ground, you can do it on their back." This was usually followed by the *thwat* as he spat some chewing tobacco into the arena soil. "Pay attention to the body, what

161

they're tellin' you. Pay attention to your body and what it's communicating to the horse."

Groundwork is mostly overlooked in many riding disciplines, as it is just one more task or chore taking time away from riding, which is where most equestrians want to direct their time and training towards. The thrill and excitement from being on the back of a horse is empowering, much like the thrill of a marriage proposal and wedding planning. Usually the path that requires more work and patience is often overlooked, but brings a greater level of peace and mastery. I was growing to love playing on the ground with the horses, building those movements and sense of connection. I never felt nervous handling the therapy horses, who were so attuned to our body language, whereas the flashy, large show-jumper horses I was interacting with at my riding lessons could make me incredibly nervous with their lack of focus and enormously athletic bodies. With more potential and momentum, they were like a spring coiled with immense energy.

There was an amusing contrast between the world I was working to fit into and the world that I brought along with me. My days working at the barn were spent being silly and playful with neurodivergent children, feeling a sense of community with their parents, volunteers and staff. Coming home to our neat, manicured gated development at night, my face would be dusted with dirt, bits of hay sticking out of my hair or pockets. The happiness in my heart glowed, reassuring me that everything was going to be okay, maybe while laughing at the contrast of my muddy Subaru to the immaculately landscaped lawns I passed.

My heart has always felt happiest in the wildness of the land or in the spirited connection that horses offered. Things were calm and content at the barn, but coming home every night was starting to feel tense and lonely. The relationship I had moved hundreds miles to preserve was tearing at the seams. William was becoming emotionally closed-up and distant. There were nights where the distance between us became so apparent that I had never felt such intense loneliness. We each increasingly began spending most of our evenings in separate areas of the house, the connection between us becoming more difficult to bridge. With the large leap outside of my comfort zone during this transition, my confidence also took a dive. At dinners with the other surgeons and their wives, I would stumble over my words, faltering when the attention became pointed at me or my career. William's family was patient and helpful, welcoming me in and aiding as I networked within the new community, but I was nervous about what was being said about me amongst themselves.

Later that fall, as the trees of the balmy hills shed their leaves to the approaching winter chill, two of my close friends in Colorado had experienced the unthinkable. The ranch managers of Mustard Seed had lost their premature baby after weeks in the NICU and a former neighbor had the certainty of raising a healthy infant shattered with the diagnosis of a rare childhood cancer. Thinking of the unbearable pain they must have been feeling, I curled around myself in bed, feeling helpless so far away and not being able to be more supportive of them during those incredibly difficult times. I saw their strength as they updated their community through texts and Facebook posts, focusing on the positives, any hope or faith they could cling to. The heaviness of their situations would linger with me for days, as I reflected on the unexpected events and sorrows that completely upend us and alter the way in which we view and participate in life. I heard many unimaginable situations and tragedies from clients and their families, but had rarely witnessed the drastic loss of a sense of normalcy in those close to me.

Around the same time, I had started working with a 14-year-old French girl at Equestrian Bridges, who had her own dreams and expectations shattered. Emmy had grown up with her family of five in France before puzzling symptoms began emerging, confusing both her parents and physicians. With a healthy and seemingly normal childhood, they couldn't understand the sudden fatigue and chronic pain Emmy was describing. The symptoms progressed where she could no longer participate in her activities or school. She was passed along to different therapy appointments and other specialists while her parents grew more and more concerned when no one had an answer. Emmy's immune system began to weaken significantly. She had a feeding tube inserted when she was no longer able to digest food and eventually needed to rely on a wheelchair as the muscles and nerves and her legs rapidly atrophied.

Without answers or hope for a cure in France, the family split their time between northwest Arkansas, where a care facility existed for teenagers like Emmy, who were diagnosed with this incredibly rare autoimmune and pain disorder. For years the family had navigated this difficult dynamic, willing to do everything and anything that could alleviate their daughter's pain or lead to a possible remission. Emmy's diagnosis upended the lives of her parents and siblings as well, as they navigated the rift that her illness and an ocean between them created.

Upon my intake lesson with Emmy, I learned she had only begun barely walking again that same week as we slowly took small steps from her wheelchair up the steps of the mounting block to approach the horse's back. Exhausted, she expressed climbing the stairs and petting the horse was enough of an exertion for her that day. The following week, with the assistance of David and our volunteer Kate, she was able to mount onto the horse's back and be guided for several laps around the indoor arena. Despite the debilitating condition I had read about from her chart, the young girl in front of me beamed with pride while she told us stories about her family, her interests in music and art, and what her dream house would look like someday. The swift emotional connection between Emmy and the horse was touching. Radiating with happiness after the ten minutes of riding she felt comfortable with, she requested to dismount and be done for the day, noting her fatigue.

The following afternoon, I was teaching a lesson in the arena when Tracey, our office administrator, appeared at the entrance and gestured eagerly to come over her. I directed the volunteers while I stepped away, keeping my eyes on the horse and rider.

"You'll never believe what just happened," she said excitedly as I approached. "You know your little girl who started riding recently?"

Confused, I tilted my head, looking at her for more context. "Emmy?"

"Yes. Well, her mother just came into the office with tears streaming down her face. She could barely talk as she said that she wanted her daughter to get into as many riding lessons as possible because last night was the first time her daughter had indicated that she hadn't felt pain in years."

Stunned, both of us had tears in our eyes, looking back at one another in disbelief. *Whoa.* We both grappled with the giddy miraculousness of it, while still reeling in disbelief. I had seen some remarkable progress over the course of several weeks or months in adaptive riding lessons and equine psychotherapy sessions, but I had never experienced a parent who had noticed such a profound difference in their child after one incredibly brief ride.

I felt reinvigorated leaving the barn that evening. I felt part of something remarkable with Emmy, the volunteers and the other staff of Equestrian Bridges. I was finally feeling rooted in the local community through my work, feeling grateful for the sense of belonging and purpose. With the fading orange sun sinking into the hills of the Ozarks, I drove home eager to share my joy with William. Things had felt fraught and fragile between us over the past few weeks with wedding planning becoming more concrete. I was relieved I could share a night where I was starting to feel genuinely hopeful and optimistic about our new home, where the tension between us could evaporate into the humid air. But sometimes life steers you into a new direction entirely, leaving you feeling blindsided and betrayed.

One April afternoon, not long after that evening after Emmy's encouraging session, William came home early from work and I was looking forward to a fun and relaxing evening. Heavy conversations around wedding planning and the growing uncertainty I was feeling from him had filled our week and we had agreed to take a small reprieve from them. When I sensed my enthusiasm was not shared, I hesitatingly asked, "How's your heart?"

His brows furrowed to tense lines of seriousness as he sighed, more frustrated than I had anticipated. "I didn't want to do this tonight." The defeat in his voice and the cold indifference on his face said it all. There was nothing to be done. With the breath of air stuck in my throat, I hesitated to breathe, wanting to freeze time. Stunned but not entirely surprised at this point, I sighed and finally conceded.

After five years of dating and seven months going through the motions of a life together in Arkansas, I knew then it was truly over. The loss of a serious relationship can feel like such an anticlimactic ending to a significant portion of your life. Despite willingness and patience, there was a piece of his heart I could never fully reach and his wavering commitment could never be soothed. And just as suddenly as time had stood at a standstill, it began to move very quickly. My pounding heart and mind began racing with questions: *Where would I go now? What happens to me?*

I called my mom in between sobs as William quickly packed. Minutes later, he paused by the door with his suitcase, apologizing one last time. Unable to meet his gaze, my stubborn pride prevented me from turning around to watch him walk out of my life for good. The remainder of that night was a blur. Hugging Tucker, I called my friends and family, continuing to ask, "What do I do?" All I could do was lie beside my dog, stroking the coarse hair of his shoulder, while tears rolled down my face.

I faded in and out of sleep before the morning sun cruelly illuminated how numb and wrung out I felt. Looking out of the window, my eyes swollen from crying and a long sleepless night, I felt that the only place for me to go was the barn. I called Shanna, knowing that I should give her a courtesy call. "Hey," I said, fighting back the lump of emotion stuck in my throat, "I'm still planning on coming in today and seeing all my clients, but I just wanted to let you know that William left me."

"WHAT?! Are you okay?"

Of course I didn't feel okay. My heart and mind were reeling with the shock that there would be no wedding, not future together. Knowing I would return to Colorado, I now had no job, no home, the loss of my closest friend and our dreams together. Yet I still felt that going through my normal routine that day would at least give me some level of distraction. I thought being in the comfort of the barn family I had developed over the past months in Arkansas would be healthy for me. I knew David, Kate and Shanna would be there and I had been able to be my authentic self with them. Horses never lie and neither do the people who cherish that most about them.

When Shanna asked if I was sure that I wanted to come to work, I reassured her, blinking back tears, "Yeah, I'll be fine." I also had undergrad interns that day and a whole roster of sessions with clients who were relying on me. I knew it would be difficult to cover those responsibilities between the staff so last minute.

Later that morning, walking into the indoor arena, I saw David stand to approach me. I felt my stomach drop, realizing how difficult this day would actually be. Crumbling, I reached out for a hug and began crying into his shoulder, "He left me."

"I know. Shanna told me," he said in his warm way.

With none of my familiar friends or family around me, I was held closely by those I had met working with the horses, representing all the best attributes of horse people—honest, compassionate, loyal and hardworking. David and Kate helped me significantly that day and watching kids ride and interact with the horses gave me comfort and hope. David even got me to laugh when he looked me dead in the eye with all seriousness and his southern sass and said, "Now, Miss Shanna was mad at me because I looked at the hospital Facebook page and wrote them a review, tellin' 'em that they had a heart surgeon there who was breakin' more hearts than he was fixin'." A *thwat* of chewing tobacco adding to his point.

I managed to go through the motions of my lessons that day, grateful for the brief moments where I forgot about the issues crumbling beneath my feet. Later that afternoon, slipping away from the arena, I spent hours standing in the paddock using a shedding blade on a handful of our gentle therapy horses. There is something very cathartic for me in brushing the dead winter hair out of a horse's coat to reveal the shiny and healthy coat underneath, a sure sign of spring approaching. The serenity of community and connection circled around me, as each horse peacefully inched forward for their turn, basking in the warmth of the sunlight. It was a relief not to have to speak a word. Their lowered heads and softened eyes reminded me that despite feeling broken, my heart was still open and recognized by those who spoke the most intuitive language. "I'll scratch your back, if you scratch mine." Or rather the lesson that has resonated strongest in Equus, "I'll open my heart to you, if you open yours to me."

Separating without knowing where that next handhold to grasp can be a terrifying experience. The separation from dreams of our future, the health of a loved one or sense of security can leave us searching, feeling an intensity with each new emotion. The pain can sit heavy in the core of our soul, while the simplest gestures of kindness brings us closer to the humanity we seemed to have lost sight of. In separation, we lose the familiarity of our security, but we also shed the preconceived notions of ourselves we had grown accustomed to.

The concept of disengagement feels messy. In the saddle, it would imply that the rider was ignoring an area of the horse's physiology, leading to poor conformation in its movement. This can be completely oblivious to a beginner or novice, but a skilled rider would feel the loss of balance, the choppiness of movement or errors in the horse's performance, for example. Learning how to engage a horse under saddle is the ultimate goal in riding. On the ground, disengagement is the skill set that feels more attuned to dancing with a partner. The horse leader has to remain relaxed and grounded, while also remaining several steps ahead mentally in their planning and timing. The horse as a partner in comparison remains fluid, adaptable to shifting their movement, despite not knowing the next move or direction.

In my lessons with David, I was learning to hone the subtlest of cues to ask a horse to step away from my pressure. Asking a horse to discontinue circling around me, I would stop the movement of my feet, tilt my head while directing my eyes towards their rump and lifting the 'leading' hand of the rope in order to ask the horse to stop forward movement and to instead, swing their hind end away from the pressure of my eyes. Standing alert now at attention facing me, the horse would lick and chew, pleased with the rest and an anticipated face rub. In the most graceful three seconds I had experienced in interacting with a horse, the movement felt almost like I was extending my arm out and presenting my dance partner to curtsey at the closure of a dance.

When my mom arrived from Colorado several days later to help me pack, Shanna graciously allowed us to stay at her lake house while we worked on separating my things again at the house, packing them into a shipping container that sat on the driveway. Leaving my key on the counter, I slipped under the garage door of what had been my home only days before.

Unbeknownst to me, at the same time while we were driving across the state lines from Arkansas to Missouri and Kansas, Emmy was about to extend an arm for a final bow in a performance of her own. David had shown her how to disengage his pinto horse Tuffy and send him cantering around her at liberty while she stood in the center of the arena. Eyes fixated on the horse's soft brown-and-white-spotted body, Emmy turned and shifted her own body, urging Tuffy towards a line of barrels that had been placed, blockading his path around the arena. In the final turn before the obstacle, Emmy beamed with excitement and began running alongside her horse, holding the pressure on him as he leapt from the ground and sailed across the barrels. The girl whose health and childhood had been taken from her by illness now ran, only four weeks after having regained the ability to begin walking again. Perhaps stumbling at first, we regain the sense of strength and balance to begin moving forward again. Through her act, Emmy had given her own final bow to her dance with pain. She would be defeated no longer.

Heading west towards Colorado with Tucker by my side, something shifted in me. With the many encouraging words and acts of love, my heart clung to the hope that someday I would be able to find my own resolution. Like a horse side-stepping away from their leader, I was hopefully surrendering, awaiting instruction in the anticipation of release from the universe in my own disengagement.

9.

Obstacles in the Right Direction

Despite my quiet and reserved nature, I'm enamored by the thrill and risk I find jumping horses over large obstacles. Having to focus on navigating the course while communicating with the animal beneath me is loud enough to silence any other thoughts. Whether riding on the back of a running horse or skiing down a mountain, there's no greater feeling than the rush associated with thrill sports; finding that space to be fully mindful of the present moment. A flow state is the experience of being so completely immersed in a particular task or activity, losing sense of time and finding freedom from stressors or our internal critic. Riding, but especially jumping, is where I find my flow state. The movement of the horse's swaying rib cage becomes synchronized with my breathing; inhale, exhale, while the adrenaline feels invigorating.

Equestrian sports are unique in that the horse beneath you has its own thoughts and behaviors that create an element of uncertainty. The training and connection we develop with our animal hopes to alleviate most risks, while building an expectation of trust in one another. Like any activity or decision, risks are a reality we have to assess and prepare for. The expression of falling off and getting back on the horse illustrates the determination and courage needed to confront something that just recently hurt or disappointed us. Falling off, getting hurt and willing to risk it again can feel like near insanity in the moment, but overcoming our fear teaches us that we also underestimate our capability. No life is free from obstacles. Some are more complicated or challenging than others, but we learn to navigate them. All we can do is brush ourselves off, learn from the past and swing back up into the saddle.

It was disappointing having put all my faith into William's word and then living with the fallout when those promises fell short. Heartbroken but determined that this breakup wouldn't impact my life any more than it already had, I began emailing every organization throughout Colorado for any opportunity working with horses therapeutically. I flipped through the three full pages of contacts I had been tracking on a legal pad without success. Now without anything holding me back, I was hopeful I could use this opportunity to relocate to the mountains in one of Colorado's ski towns, dreaming of either Crested Butte or Telluride. The shock of losing the certainty of an entire life you've planned on also brings the freedom to start fresh and build the future you've always wished for.

Weeks later and still not finding any solid work in Colorado, an opportunity I had seen on a job-posting website located in Montana stuck with me. It advertised a high salary at a facility that promoted wellness and nature-based therapies in a dreamy location. After two months of exhausting every option in Colorado, I decided it might be worthwhile to contact the director of this facility. I emailed back and forth with Karen and was able to do a video interview with several staff members. She assured me that the salary was accurate and that mental health resources were so limited in the area that they always had a lengthy waitlist of clients and had struggled to recruit a therapist with the necessary credentials.

Two weeks later, feeling that the opportunity was legitimate, I took the risk and flew over the patchwork quilt of the plains, the endless yellow and brown squares interrupted only by the green circles of the irrigation pivots. On our descent over the glacial-blue alpine lakes and pine-studded mountain ranges, I felt hopeful of potentially fulfilling a childhood dream of working with horses in Montana. I thought back to the manila envelope stuffed full of childhood blueprints for my dream ranch and smiled at the serendipity of it all.

Landing in Kalispell, a small city in northwestern Montana, just on the doorstep of Glacier National Park, I was eager to explore the job opportunity and local communities. Despite some initial hesitation at the promised position, I was impressed by the structure of the organization. They had an office manager who scheduled and aided with insurance billing, maintained electronic records, and had a well-established intake process for new clients. I asked Karen and the other staff about their practice and clients, while also inquiring about the local culture. I was immediately drawn to living in the quaint town of Whitefish. There was a ski mountain and I felt it might be easier to be more social and to connect with people my age in an active resort town. I was set to meet a landlord to view a townhouse that was within walking distance of the downtown.

Everything seemed to be falling into place that weekend, except the cold and distant energy from Meg, the other therapist on site. She was not willing to let me shadow any of her sessions and clearly wasn't enthusiastic about me joining. Looking for any source for her hostility, I asked if I would be removing clients from her caseload. I was desperate for income, stability and a fresh start. I wanted this opportunity to be my new landing place, but was still looking for the catch in this too-good-to-be-true opportunity. I reasoned perhaps it was a reflection of something personal to her and vowed to keep my head down and ignore it for the time being. Leaving that week, I smiled with the blooming optimism of this new chapter of my life. I had committed to the therapy position, secured the townhouse in Whitefish and began planning the logistics of moving my belongings from the shipping container to Montana.

In early July, with the enthusiasm and thrill of taking this big leap, I started the morning of my first day of work, when the entire staff was called together for a team meeting. I still felt a little exhausted from the difficult move. After the 16-hour drive, my stuff had been delayed three additional days and I had spent several nights sleeping on the floor of the townhouse before my furniture arrived. Sitting down in the cool, concrete tack room, I realized that something serious was taking place. Meg, the other therapist, initiated the discussion by making her resignation official. *Good riddance*, I initially thought. As she continued that Karen had been committing unethical billing practices by billing for sessions that a licensed therapist had not conducted, or billing individual rates when the session was run as a group with multiple participants, my heart seized. Both Meg and I were unlicensed therapists practicing under Karen's license—this was an extremely detrimental allegation. Not only is insurance fraud illegal, everyone involved would have their license to practice revoked, regardless of whether or not they knew of the unethical billing practices. Jaw hanging, I felt God was playing a terrible joke on me. If this information was true, I would have to resign immediately. Karen became tearful, claiming her own supervisor had shown her this billing practice and she didn't know any better. Stunned by the conflicting stories, I didn't know what to believe.

After the meeting, I felt the gut-punch feeling of betrayal rising and confronted Meg by the gate of a horse pasture. During my initial visit, I had disclosed to these women the circumstances around why I was seeking employment and relocating. How could she not tell me this information *before* I accepted the job, *before* I relocated yet again away from my entire support system. All that I was seeking was to reestablish a sense of security for myself and the immediate future. Meg maintained the accusations were correct, but offered little sympathy with my situation. I approached the other administrative and facility staff, who cryptically confirmed my fears, and alluded to considering resigning themselves. Trying to comprehend the situation and my options, there were days that I could do little more than cry on the floor. I wanted to be okay and needed some glimmer of hope after the immense pain and humiliation of my engagement ending. I had been so hopeful that this position would provide the stability I needed, while simultaneously offering a fresh new adventure in Montana. Any tiny scrap of hope or optimism that I had carefully gathered mending my broken heart now scattered, ripped from my hands.

But each day offered a new opportunity and slowly out of a survival drive, I made efforts and considered my options. Searching online, I saw that I was eligible to become licensed in Montana, which was never something I had considered before. Every state has different requirements for psychotherapists and Montana's were much more lenient than Colorado's. I would need to pass my licensure exam and begin accruing hours and letters of recommendations from former supervisors.

Exploring the valley, as the locals called it, I began looking for new horse facilities. I dropped flyers off at local arenas, tack stores, private barns—anywhere I felt someone might be willing to let me lease space and horses for my own business. Encountering other equine professionals, I was reassured of my decision to resign from the organization I moved there for. Apparently, this had been an ongoing issue for several years and many other local therapists had been hurt by her business and billing practices. I felt duped again by another horse organization that promised incredible opportunities to young professionals who relied on the facilities and horses they provided, only to become a financial pawn by the owner for their own gain.

I balanced my time studying for licensure and setting up my business with exploring the gorgeous Montana summer. The days were long, the vegetation lush, and the community was so friendly and encouraging. Tucker and I would start our mornings at the local dog park or swimming beach on the lake, with the ski mountain rising in the background, where I socialized with retirees and families who encouraged my efforts and offered suggestions for people I should contact or connect with. The relief of having a supportive new community around me helped push me through those first difficult days and months. I felt *seen* and comforted by genuine compassion from strangers, reinstilling some faith in others. I tried to remain hopeful, reminding myself that these obstacles would lead me on a different path, one that would be more fulfilling.

Having given up the security of my salaried position at Mustard Seed, I had run through any savings and needed to scrape together some money while I worked at starting my own practice. For months the yellow diamond had remained hidden in the clutches of the wooden box it came in and I knew I couldn't justify holding on to it any longer. The ring, the final reminder of future dreams that it had symbolized, had lost its value to me. The kindness of a local jeweler reassured me that they happened to know the perfect gentleman looking to surprise his girlfriend with something truly unique. Relieved, I hoped that my loss would become a treasure in someone else's story, while it bought me more time in Montana as I worked at becoming more established.

I continued emailing local stables and fortuitously made contact with Kat and Sally of a local therapeutic riding center called Two Bear and was invited to their facilities for an introduction. Driving along the dusty country road past the rows of cut and drying hay on the hundreds of acres of fields felt soothingly hypnotic. The rows curved with the landscape like the evenly raked lines of a Zen garden. The immaculately maintained property had paddocks full of grazing horses—beautiful buckskins, chestnuts and bays—tucked under clusters of tamarack and lodgepole pines before opening up into expansive meadows and mountains on the horizon.

Stopping her chores on the riding lawn mower, Kat, a thin, striking green-eyed women in her late twenties, with her long, blonde hair flung over one shoulder, enthusiastically greeted me and gave me a hug. She led me up to the stately brown wooden barn. Several cattle dogs barked at the intrusion of a new visitor as we stepped inside among the rows of saddle racks with individualized tooled-leather name tags.

A spritely, mustached cowboy, nearing sixty, in boots and denim, peered over his coffee cup at me and nodded. "How's it going?"

Kat introduced me by name and credentials, mentioning I was looking for work and facilities where I could do equine psychotherapy sessions. Eager for an open door, I said half-jokingly, "I'm even happy to pick stalls if you need it!"

Chuckling from his seat, Mitch asked, "You think we keep any horses in these stalls?"

Looking around I saw that in addition to the elk-horn chandelier in the entryway, the expansive horse stalls were used as feed and tack rooms rather than housing horses. The polished barn interior looked more like a hotel lobby than a stable. Kat introduced me to her mother Sally, equally striking and slim, with her long, greying hair pulled into a braid that ran down the length of her back. Continuing the tour with the indoor arena and horse pastures, Kat offered to go on a trail ride. Mitch and Sally joined us and led me out across the hay fields and alongside the winding river. Feeling my saddle slip slightly when I had first mounted from the ground, I stood in my stirrups and jerked the saddle to the right, hoping to recenter it. Embarrassed I had not addressed it immediately, I hoped this action would go unnoticed, but I heard Mitch chuckle behind me. "I was wondering when you were going to fix that." Smiling, I reasoned I had survived the stubborn sass of David's obsessive attention to detail, I figured I could manage the scrutiny of another cowboy.

When the achingly long days of summer receded and with it the crowds of tourists, the valley had a more sinister underbelly that grew in the stillness. Social interaction became more limited to either outdoor recreation or drinking at a local bar. Rates of alcoholism, suicide and domestic violence in Montana were among the nation's highest.

"What are you running from?" was the pointed response when I shared that I had recently moved to Whitefish and that question held a great deal of truth. Many people were looking to escape when they came to Montana, whether from society, a broken heart, a failed business—people like me who were seeking a fresh start. Those hardened hearts grew more determined but perhaps with a heaviness from the loss of hope, much like the rocky and frozen landscape surrounding us as it became harsher and more desolate throughout winter. I began frequently encountering many women both as clients and within the community who had experienced varying degrees of violence and unhealthy relationships, spanning a variety of socioeconomic levels. The escape and solitude that Montana offered also brought with it the lack of oversight and desperately needed resources for its population. As a mental health professional providing a unique therapy intervention in working with horses, the interest in my practice thrived from the beginning. I didn't have to sell how horses were therapeutic. Everyone here already knew.

My first client in Montana was Julia, a woman who had fled from a toxic relationship. After an argument had escalated, her alcoholic partner had left bruising on her arm and the cops had become involved. Julia had spent the previous winter hiking and camping in Glacier National Park alone, using a local gym for a hot shower, not sure which direction to turn. However bleak that scenario may sound, she was far from destitute. Her natural exuberance and gratitude for life spilled out of her energetic and smiling face. Formerly a barrel racer in her teenage years, she was drawn towards my work to form a relationship with a horse again while processing her conflicting relationship.

Often when people have betrayed our trust and left us feeling flighty, animals can begin to fill the voids of our heart that ache for connection. Julia was immediately drawn towards Biggie, a handsome buckskin gelding, who had experienced his own trauma. As a well-bred roping horse, Biggie landed in the hands of men who saw him as a new toy and rode him hard; causing a deep muscle tear in his shoulder that left him stiff and hobbling, but overall sound enough for very light therapeutic riding or groundwork. By the time Two Bear began working with Biggie in their therapeutic riding center, he was fairly dissociated most of the time and nervous about being saddled. To him, being ridden was associated with the severe pain that was ignored by his former riders.

Much like humans or any other animals, horses can be traumatized into a dissociative or completely checked-out state. There is a training technique known as 'tie down' where a horse is laid on its side using ropes and the handler lies on the horse's side until it submits and appears settled. This technique had been described to me by a horse trainer in the past and sounded staggeringly cruel, but they reassured me that it was peaceful and remarkable to see the difference in their temperament. Unfortunately, that is definitely not the case. From a horse's perspective, lying on their side with a predator pressed on top of them literally means they are going to die.

When a prey animal is caught by a predator, their brain releases neurochemicals that aid in the acceptance of imminent death. Only if they were to escape and flee, would their bodies begin to tremble and physically process the miracle that they had survived. Tying down a horse imprints that highly traumatized state where death feels certain, without allowing them to physically flee or tremble as their instincts would compel them to do in the wild. Much like a human who has been physically restrained or held against their will, these dissociated animals become socially removed from the herd, unable to engage in nurturing relationships or express themselves freely. As the lowest-ranking member of the herd, Biggie exhibited all of these characteristics in addition to restless head tossing and backing when tied for grooming. Many of the women I worked with during that time who had experienced violence or a manipulative partner were drawn towards Biggie. Perhaps there is something crying out to be simultaneously nurtured in them by caring for an animal who can too closely relate to their traumatic experience.

Anyone who has worked with an animal, child or person who has experienced physical trauma knows it is a patient process peeling back the layers one at a time. The timing and progression is always in the hands of the client or animal. Sometimes it is the first element of their lives they have had control of.

Julia was forthcoming about the night that had led to her partner's arrest and how she had stayed by his side throughout the trial. At the time, she had found stable housing in Montana, but visited her partner occasionally on weekends back in Washington. In addressing someone from an abusive relationship, it's important to remember that there are reasons they stay, reasons they are attracted to their partner. Sometimes it is practical such as children, finances or other resources. And other times there are the remnants of passion, promises of change or simply glimpses of feeling loved in a harsh world. All humans and animals have an innate need to feel valued and loved by others.

Over our sessions together, Julia shared details of a relationship that was seemingly social and lovely on the outside, but tormented and manipulative behind closed doors. There were nights her partner would become so intoxicated that he wandered on the frozen lake behind their home, threatening suicide and leaving her pleading on the shore for him to come back inside. She admitted that the fear of finding him dead or him hurting himself suspended her in a state of helplessness where she was unable to tend to her own basic needs. As the months passed, I began to notice a change in her demeanor and motivation after returning from a visit with him in Washington. It was obvious he had a hold over her that was inhibiting her from moving forward and living a life free of the emotional terror he created.

During one of her sessions, hoping to encourage her to open up, I told her a story about a team of scientists who were trying to capture a highly elusive primate that they had never studied in captivity. "The monkey had evaded each entrapment they set. One of the researchers had observed how much the monkey enjoyed the fresh fruit they had used as bait, especially the oranges. He shared his idea and constructed a simple box that would be filled with oranges. They dug a small hole next to the box that was just wide enough for the monkey to insert his hand up into the box, but not wide enough that he could pull his arm back out while clutching onto the fruit. The scientists were able to capture the monkey because he was unwilling to release his precious reward. He was entirely free to leave sitting on the outside of the entrapment, but he had ensnared himself with short-sightedness of his desire by continuing to clutch onto the orange."

Julia smiled at the story, catching on to what I was implying with her relationship. The next week that I saw her, she happily confided that she had been eating an orange every morning thinking about that story and what it meant for her. During the following weeks of our sessions grooming Biggie, where both he and Julia would become grounded and regulated, she admitted the fear of being alone prevented her from severing her relationship.

After seven months of weekly therapy sessions, Julia was able to identify the recurring cycle in the relationship and his alcoholism that prevented any real change from taking place. She began setting boundaries with the time she spent with him, prioritizing herself and other friendships during her visits in Washington. While she was away, I received an email from Julia, reassured of the progress she was making: *You are definitely one-of-a-kind and you treat me as one-of-a-kind. Because of that, I feel comfortable talking to you, and my healing process has started.*

Using traffic cones, ground poles, rings, pool noodles and other accessories, I will instruct a client to create an obstacle course for them to lead their horse through. "But that obstacle course has to reflect a personal obstacle you're also going through in your own life," I would add, sometimes to an eyeroll response. Essentially, this activity becomes experiential in the way the client creates physical representation of the inner conflict and emotions they're experiencing. Sometimes they will make a square with the four ground poles when they feel trapped, or conversely, the square can become a refuge in a chaotic environment. Clusters of traffic cones become a difficult and overwhelming maze of emotions or obligations. Within reason, I allow the construction process to be as creative as possible, as the point is not necessarily to create a fully-functional obstacle course.

They walk me through the physical course paralleled with what each obstacle represents in their situation. Without judgment and as long as the course is safe, they are free to begin leading their horse through. The most common practical error is placing the traffic cones or obstacles too close together, where the horse is unable to turn as narrowly as their leader anticipated. Horses will also intentionally avoid stepping on items the client had lain out with that objective. After the initial bumpy first round, I'll ask, "Okay, so how did that go?" Aware of the difficulties they encountered, I then offer, "So, if you could remove or add one item to make it easier, what would you do?" They may remove an obstacle that was too challenging, or place items to be navigated around, rather than stepped on. Their second time through the course will go smoother and we discuss how we cannot dwell on the past, only learn from it.

With the one-year mark approaching our time working together, I instructed Julia to create an obstacle course representing her journey. She gladly accepted the vague instructions and began pulling out ground poles and barrels, placing them around the arena. Finished, we stood back to admire the series of obstacles. Julia began with three ground poles she had placed up against the side of the arena forming a box, representing her relationship and time in Washington. She walked around two barrels forming a figure-eight pattern, explaining that was the time she was 'circling', not sure what move to make or which direction to go. She then led Biggie to the oversized soccer ball that sometimes a willing horse would paw at or playfully bite. "This is me kicking around real ideas," she explained before nudging it towards the 'goal' at the end of the area. Her goal was visiting Hawaii someday.

"Excellent! I love it," I said as we headed back to the beginning, ready to lead Biggie through the challenge. "I'm curious though why you built the box of poles using the wall and not out in the middle of the arena."

Holding the lead rope in her hands, she stood with Biggie in the box. I saw her smile fade over the next few seconds and her eyes shifted to the dirt at her feet. When she finally met my gaze, I could hear the tone of emotion in her throat, "I guess I felt like my back was up against the wall."

In constructing a simple representation of a tumultuous relationship, Julia was able to enact feelings and an understanding of the circumstances that led her there. We are all able to reflect in hindsight on certain events in our lives, but it's important to meet them without judgment. We are usually compelled into relationships and decisions in the hope that our life will improve with time and patience. Perspective on the factors surrounding those decisions allows us to empathize with our younger selves; we were doing what we knew and what we thought was best, even if it didn't turn out the way that we had hoped. I was still disappointed that my engagement didn't end in marriage and embarrassed that I uprooted my life on William's flimsy promises. But I never would have ended up in Montana had our relationship not fallen apart. I was angry at Karen and her riding center for not being the ethical and stable employment

I needed, but I never would have started my own therapy practice at Two Bear had my own back not been pressed against the wall.

Several months later, I received a postcard from Julia in Hawaii depicting a stunning sliver of palm-fringed shoreline, where she'd had gone to break free, to define herself anew: *Aloha! I have been here since New Year's Eve and loving the fact that this dream would have never come true unless our paths crossed.*

Sometimes the obstacles on our path—seemingly disastrous, disruptive or difficult to navigate—happen to be leading us in the right direction. It's also a reminder that resilience and perseverance can often to lead our greatest successes.

10.

The Square

The Flathead Valley is cradled by sloping mountains on all sides, with the daunting crests of Glacier peeking from behind the walls of the canyon towards the northeast. To be held so close to nature, my heart rested in the peaceful reminder that everything has a season. Each frigid blizzard thaws with the warm rains of spring, and to every dark night, a promising dawn. In Montana summers, anything feels possible. Grassy green pastures stretch for miles with the yellow fields of canola flowering in late June, contrasting the deep blue skies. Billowing gold castles of clouds tower overhead, subsiding late into the night before the shower of stars began to emerge. Spotted fawns nurse from their mothers while flights of hummingbirds dive and skitter through the aspen groves in search of nectar. The summers, a rich bounty after having lasted the many dark months of winter, are magical but brief.

Just as the summer emerges from the monsoon rains of June, it subsides again into the chilly fog and gloom of November. Feeling the warmth of the sun between November and February is rare in northwest Montana. The endless grey days of winter test your mental and emotional stamina. At worst, pressing claustrophobia and depression creep in, if not mindfully tempered through social engagement and outdoor recreation. Yet hibernation can also be a welcomed refuge from the short days and frozen landscape to intentionally withdraw for a period of reflection and rest.

After having disrupted the flow of your life by loss, hurt or heartache, you can feel entitled to an upcoming fortuitous event. I found motivation in the hopes that I would soon meet a magnificent partner that would justify any heartache I had endured. Despite feeling slightly hesitant and fragile, I approached dating with renewed determination. The only problem was there weren't too many viable options to be found in rural Montana. Those times were countered by periods where I truly immersed myself in the contentment of the routine I had established between my therapy practice, interspersed with hiking and lake trips with Tucker, skiing, horseback riding and spending time with the group of friends I had developed. I had so much to be grateful for and felt the relief and sense of pride in myself for pushing through a particularly dark period. My faith in finding a partner wavered like the push-pull of the seasons. Sometimes it felt suffocating or daunting and other times I basked in the abundance already surrounding me.

The square is an activity I love to use after a few sessions with someone, where they are just comfortable enough working with a horse, but still relatively inexperienced. Using four ground poles or cones, I will construct a square in the middle of the arena, approximately eight to ten feet on all four sides. Giving intentionally vague instructions, I set the horse loose in the arena and tell the client that their challenge is to move the horse inside the square, and once there, get it to stand still, all without touching it. They usually stare back at me in confusion for several seconds where I imagine they are internally questioning whether this whole 'horse therapy' approach is right for them.

Whether working as a group or individual, I gain enormous insight from this activity into how a client approaches a challenge. Most individuals typically start by calling to the horse like a dog, hopeful that it will obediently follow them. The unresponsive horse, typically shut down in a relaxed state with its head dropped and ears turned out to the side, indicates to the disappointed client that they will have to try a different approach. The horse is not ignoring the client, as they might assume, simply waiting for more intentional instruction. As long as the attempts remain safe for both the participant and the horse, I encourage whatever approach they come up with, no matter how silly or ill-conceived. I have watched clients gently kick the arena sand at the horse's legs, bribe with promises of grass, jump up and down, or try to pull the horse along with an invisible rope.

Observing group dynamics is much more interesting. I immediately see which member takes initiative and which ones shrink to the outside of the circle. I also see when a group is working against itself. For example, when participants are on either side of the horse urging it to move away from them, not recognizing their peers are on the other side are attempting the same strategy. Defeated, they stare back at me hopeful for a clue. I urge them to reconsider information I fed to them in their initial first sessions. Horses move *away* from pressure. They may start to raise and wave their arms above their head—they've at least gotten the horse's attention. Now walking towards the horse with this pressure, the horse begins stepping away, hoping to relieve themselves from the uncomfortable sensation of being approached with that intensity.

Once the animal is moving, the person can relax their body language and simply has to guide the horse in the intended direction. They walk from behind or the side, steering the horse with pressure from the left if they want it to move right, or back off if they want the horse to stop or slow down. Quickly they have picked up the non-verbal herding communication that horses use to direct one another in a herd or to indicate who is more dominant. Horses use this intention and pressure behind their movement to shove a lesser-ranking herd member away from the desired pile of hay, conveying the hierarchy of social structure within the herd. We as humans may misinterpret this behavior as aggression or bullying, but this is simply the easiest and most effective way to communicate with one another and maintain social structure within the herd. In working with horses, it is necessary to learn the horse's natural language of using our bodies to direct and set boundaries to continue to maintain the peace and remind them that we will not be pushed around or dominated when we are interacting with them.

After a client has learned the 'herding' approach of using pressure to move the horse away from them, they can then soften and begin to play with the 'following' aspect of join-up, or having the horse willingly follow them towards the square. Once you have established your role as the leader in a herd, the horse defers to your judgment that you will guide them along safely and with their best interest in mind. Just a little bit of pressure is sometimes necessary to get their attention, before they peacefully follow your footsteps.

When heavy snowfall had blanketed the hay fields and the horses of Two Bear had grown their long, shaggy coats, I asked a relatively new client to participate in the square activity. Caitlin gravitated towards the equine psychotherapy approach I offered at Two Bear as an animal lover herself, having owned a horse as a teenager. Late one morning, after initially greeting Caitlin in the barn lobby, I was immediately struck by her tall, lithe body and eager energy, reflected her in wide blue eyes and huge smile.

I invited Caitlin to meet Boomer, who was tied and waiting in the indoor arena. I instructed her on how to greet a horse and lead her through grooming, both of which were intended to help emotionally and physically ground her energy. Over the next few weeks while icicles continued to drip from the barn roof outside, she disclosed more about her background and the reasons she was currently seeking therapy. Despite living a healthy, well-informed lifestyle, Caitlin seemingly couldn't attract a partner, financial stability or happiness. With a fulfilling career, confidence in her independence and judgment, she reasoned she could approach the obstacle of not having a partner both logistically and sometimes even spiritually to find a solution. Her patience and determination wavered more dramatically, often spiraling into self-pity and placing blame on any perceived flaw within herself. She also longed to be a mother more than anything. Approaching her late-thirties, she was growing increasingly anxious with the fear of racing against her biological clock.

I introduced the square activity by turning her favorite horse loose in the damp indoor arena and told Caitlin she had to get Boomer into the square without touching him. Flicking her long, dark-blonde hair over one shoulder and smiling back over towards the horse, she fawned, hoping to draw Boomer over towards her. Boomer didn't reciprocate her lovestruck gaze. The arthritic quarter horse took the opportunity to shift his weight into his right hip and begin taking a snooze. Stamping her foot, Caitlin stammered, "Boomer!" her playful indignation caused us both to smile.

I watched Caitlin problem-solve, slapping her hands on her thighs to get the drowsing horse's attention, circling behind him and repeating the action again hoping to startle him forward. Boomer's butt muscles flinched briefly as he raised his head, slightly surprised from the noise behind him, but was unwilling to move a single hoof forward. Her eyebrow arched upward and I could tell she was slightly irritated that she wasn't succeeding at this activity. Similarly, Caitlin had exhaustingly tried every dating website and app available, with the most recent hopeful guy ghosting her after their third date. Her confidence was thin. So I offered that she might have to move her energy upward, without any hesitation in herself, to encourage Boomer, who was too content to enjoy a nap in the heated indoor arena, free from the icy landscape outside.

"Come on, Boomer!" she snapped, clapping her hands with irritation. Startled to attention, Boomer began moving forward, his eyes widening in confusion. Following behind him with her energy still raised, Caitlin continued to put the pressure on his movement. After taking several strides, the horse broke into a speedy walk, hoping to move away from the intrusion and moved well past the four cones until he was safely in the far corner of the arena. Stopping midway at the square, Caitlin stared across the arena at Boomer, who was licking and chewing, eyes still wide with incredulousness from the outburst in energy.

"Okay, so how do we then drop the energy well in advance of the cones to get him to land there?" I asked, also somewhat surprised by Caitlin's emotions coming out.

Working to get him out of the corner, Caitlin chose to approach Boomer from the side, pointing her arm the direction she intended him to go while using her other arm to wave some pressure at his hind end. The now-alert Boomer walked forward, but was unwilling to soften closer to Caitlin or the cones planted between them. Several attempts were made to get Boomer away from the safety of the perimeter of the area, despite Caitlin lowering her energy and taking deep breaths to cue the horse to soften as well. Much like the task of finding a partner and starting a family, the seemingly simple activity of herding Boomer into the cones escalated with more failed attempts.

I knew feelings of rejection were likely surfacing for her. After years of former unhealthy relationships, Caitlin had worked diligently to be more aware of the qualities she was seeking in a partner, while also working to build confidence in herself. She had gone through years of therapy to address childhood wounds, prioritized a healthy lifestyle and relationships with friends and maintained a successful career, always furthering her knowledge and growth. Yet, on those lonely Montana winter nights, she would ruminate in feeling incomplete without a sense of purpose from having a family of her own. Feeling insecure and powerless to attract what and whom she desired, she would focus on her appearance, spending frivolously on a new wardrobe or another aesthetic procedure for a temporary boost in self-esteem. She also consulted with psychics and focused on methods to manifest her partner and future child, willing it to be with desperation.

There is only so much that can be approached logically, sometimes elements of luck and timing are at play too. That afternoon with Caitlin, we paused to talk about the rejection she felt in her romantic life, the frustration that the universe had yet to deliver her a family. I explored with her that she was taking the horse's refusal to join-up with her personally, "You're also feeling rejected by Boomer today."

"Yeah! I just feel like he listens to me so well every other week, I thought he would follow me right over," she replied, her misty eyes watching Boomer.

"You realize it was –10 degrees last night and he just had his breakfast. He is *stoked* to be inside the warm barn away from the other horses. In fact, it also says a lot about how safe he feels around us if he's willing to try to catch some sleep."

With that, Caitlin smiled. The point I was trying to make is that there are so many factors beyond our awareness and control that it's wasted energy to take the actions of others personally. Running low on time, I encouraged Caitlin to spend the rest of the hour grooming Boomer. He welcomed the peace and affection, while she was able to regain that sense of connection and feeling valued by the horse. I suggested that we could try the square again the following week. I couldn't offer a solution to women like Caitlin who were stuck focused on the one lacking element they so desperately yearned for. But much like focusing on the metallic grey skies and frozen fingers and toes during winter, focusing on the issue only causes internal suffering. I hoped to prevent the spiral of rejected affection that caused Caitlin to pick at herself and spend her money recklessly.

Nothing productive or beneficial would come from that mentality.

During our next session with a different headspace and perspective, Caitlin easily directed a more willing and relaxed Boomer into the square with very little initial pressure. She learned how to use her voice to clarify a request, separating it from the more explosive demands of frustration and rejection. She would have preferred completing the activity by having Boomer follow her compliantly into the square, much like the hopeful first few dates to be her soulmate, reassuring the attachment and acceptance she longed for.

There is something about having to raise our hands and energy to send the horse away from us first that we hope to avoid. Human attachment is fearful of separation, especially for those who have faced abandonment or rejection. With an animal or partner with limited communication, we are stuck trying to guess how and when to remain firm and planted, when we need to soften and allow, and sometimes when we need to take a step back and start over.

I enjoy the square because each interaction is new. There is no one singular way of doing it. Much like dating, sometimes people meet the love of their life early on, and for others it can be a frustratingly long dance with lots of ups and downs. During the next few months of sessions, Caitlin established a stronger sense of confidence in herself with an ability to reduce high expectations from initial dates and address the fear of communicating her preferences with a partner. Her attempts were no longer viewed as failures, but opportunities to reflect and redirect with a different approach.

During my second summer in Montana, I started looking for a horse to lease, hoping to grow deeper roots through the local horse community. I was connected to a woman who was looking to lease one of her geldings and I met Cal several days later. The hulking dark bay thoroughbred lifted his head above the hay he had been munching on in his pasture, assessing me with a curiosity that almost seemed to be asking, 'So what's your deal?' He had a gentle and curious demeanor, and, despite being 18 years old and a bit of a lawn ornament, his build was still sleek and athletic. As a former racehorse, Cal had been raced several times before becoming a pleasure hunter-jumper. I watched the affectionate manner in which he explored his owner Jamie, as she continued to tell me pieces of his scattered past.

When Jamie found him abandoned years ago while she was still living in California, Cal had been confined to his box stall day in and day out for over a year. Without interaction or handling, he had become neurotic and difficult to handle. Taking pity on the neglected horse, Jamie began caring for Cal. Knowing the importance of groundwork and natural horsemanship, she worked on exercises that helped focus his attention on her gentle commands while simultaneously building trust with her. After first developing a patient connection with Cal on the ground, his anxiety and destructive outbursts lessened and Jamie was able to start riding him again, giving him an outlet and sense of purpose.

I agreed to lease Cal and learned more through the other boarders at the stables, as they shared stories with me from when he first moved into the barn in Montana a few years prior. Cal had an unrelenting fear of being confined. Cross ties and box stalls could send him jigging around, weaving, or at worst fighting against the restraints in panic until he was able to break the ties with enough force. On several occasions, he had reared back in fear while still tied to the wall and losing his balance, fell back over on himself. While his fear could be destructive, he was mostly a sweet and compliant horse. For the past year, Cal had been spending his time relaxing in the pasture with the other geldings, as Jamie grew busy with her other horses and teenage kids. Much like Redwind and Buster, I was always a hopeless sucker for the overlooked, sweet gelding.

Tucker accompanied me to the barn, but he was more interested in getting to know the other women there and not the large animal I insisted on spending so much time with. I adored interacting with Cal, but was still slightly nervous leading him. He would occasionally spook at nothing with a huge outburst. But rather than fleeing away from me, he would jump or pivot into my body, despite standing firm and attempting to block him by raising my arms. Having an animal whose shoulder stood at six-feet tall and weighed 1,200 pounds jump into my lap, sent my heart into my throat. I never felt entirely safe enough to let my guard down while leading, grooming or riding him. But when he was settled, he would self-soothe by licking the post or wall near where he was tied, like a toddler with a lollipop, eagerly waiting for a peppermint treat or ear rubs.

I was grateful that my therapy practice sustained a lifestyle that gave just enough allowance to justify filling the horse-sized hole in my heart. While I could one day feel simultaneously proud of my self-growth and confidence, many nights would end with fear and uncertainty gnawing in my stomach that it was never enough. I still wanted to feel settled with a home and a partner and would grow panicked when I felt the scarcity of time or options. Why did it happen so easily for others, but not for me? Hoping to invite in abundance, sometimes our fixation on the lack can be repellant of what we're searching for. Greeting Cal in the pasture with the other geldings, I would feel those fears and nagging loneliness immediately lift when his dark, soulful eyes made contact with mine. Brushing the hair and dust from his sheen coat, I imagined the anxieties from the growing obligations from my practice, ceaseless chores at home and the emotional stress of an unknown future lifting along with it, free to linger in the sunlight of the barn before settling elsewhere.

After months of building trust and stamina through conditioning rides with Cal, I was eager to see progress in performance during our jumping lessons. I would feel discouraged with both of our sluggish abilities despite our training effort. I would especially become frustrated when Cal's headspace was on another planet with no explanation. The corner we had ridden past a thousand times suddenly sent him snorting and side-stepping, or a familiar barn cat caused him to break his tie and flee from the barn, sabotaging any hope for a ride that afternoon. Racehorses have been selectively bred for hundreds of years for their incredibly fast reaction times. Thoroughbreds are known for their athleticism, not their stoicism. While the human mind is goal-oriented, a horse's mind is sensory-based from stimulation in their environment. When a horse becomes fixated on a perceived threatening sensation, the rider has to be patient in redirecting their energy and attention to prevent a larger

211

reaction. While it may not be the clear and direct path you were hoping for, sometimes the situation calls to readjust your expectations or strategy.

In time, the long thaw of winter subsided into the mist and rain of spring and I grew excited and nervous with the upcoming first jumping competition with Cal. Without ever having loaded him in a trailer before, I set the expectation low, even if we made it to the arena several miles away, I would be happy. Moving a horse away from their familiar environment into a busy and stimulating new one can be overwhelming to many horses. With a pasture mate on the trailer next to him for company, Cal loaded with minimal hesitation and excitedly stepped off the trailer at the showgrounds 20 minutes later. With his large dark head raised, eyes wide, his nostrils snorted and blew as he surveyed the scene in front of him, before I placed some hay in front of him as a distraction. In between small bites of hay, he continued to watch the movement of other horses and trucks coming and going around him, and remained non-reactive as I began tacking him with his saddle and bridle.

Despite the chilly mist that morning, I was cautiously optimistic leading Cal towards the arena. After mounting him and doing some warm-up activities with our trainer Jen, I waited near the arena listening to hear our number called. Suddenly my sluggish horse was eagerly pacing around the entrance of the arena as I worked at distracting him with movement, slightly fearful he may bolt and send me flying off.

It was finally time for our ride. By this point, my anxiety was ready to have the anticipation and class finished so I could dismount and let Cal rest in the stall. With groups of friends, other boarders, clients and my trainer observing, I was also nervous about something embarrassing happening, like Cal running wild around the course or refusing a jump at the last second and sending me flying over his ears. But something about the energy at the show triggered Cal's memories of performing in his former career and he flew around the jumps with laser focus, meeting all the distances of the jumps smoothly and swapping his cantering leads without me asking. I surrendered to Cal's energy and enthusiasm, while I guided him to each painted fence on the course. Exhausted but relieved, we left the arena beaming with pride.

Heidi, the local tack store owner who was volunteering at the show that morning, stopped me at the gate. "I am *so* happy you two found one another," she said, tears sparkling in her eyes. "He really needed someone." My chest swelled with the sincerity of her words and I rubbed Cal's neck in appreciation. As a rider and animal lover herself, she too knew that the relational dynamic extends both ways.

Back at his show stall, Cal was content to enjoy his hay bag while I removed his saddle and reflected on our round. As friends came to congratulate us, I had to laugh with the surprise of his eagerness and at my short-sightedness. Everything I had been working painstakingly on for months, he already knew. I had surrendered to the thought that Cal was too old or unwilling to learn more advanced skills, but he had proved me wrong and addressed a limitation within myself. Hypervigilant horses take extreme patience in training them to stay present and direct their attention towards their handler. I realized I had been too eager to start jumping with a horse again and had overlooked more groundwork gaining Cal's trust and attention that would have alleviated my fears in leading a horse with unpredictable and explosive anxiety. Had I not become so rigidly focused on or exasperated from the lack of performance I felt during our lessons, I could've learned something much more valuable from this horse instead.

We took home the second-place ribbon that afternoon of our first show, when only that morning I would've felt accomplished if Cal had just loaded onto the trailer. In adjusting my expectations around a looming fear of chaos, I was thrilled with every mark of progress Cal made beyond that. Much like Caitlin and the square, there are times when it's necessary to throw all our knowledge and training at an issue, times to consult a friend or an expert, and times just to allow it to be and wait for more information. Acknowledging a fear doesn't eliminate it, but rather equalizes the power and control you maintain as well. In avoidance of fear, we react emotionally, much like Cal thrashing at his restraints, desperate to break free from the mountain lion he is certain that is crouched behind him. For many of us, the mountain lion can be the fear of ending up alone. Despite the pride in our independence and the freedom to create our own lifestyle, we are still susceptible to the strong pulls of feeling incomplete without a meaningful relationship.

Timing is perhaps the most fulfilling and most painful lesson we have to learn while navigating this complicated and beautiful life. We can become lodged in an autopilot mindset, constantly jumping from one task to the next, if we don't find moments to be more fully aware. Without moments of pause and reflection, we can miss the lesson before us. Just as with nature, there are seasons within our own lives and certain elements are on their own trajectory, no matter how much we wish to invite them in. There are those people who we feel that just seem to have things happen for them, but I feel the better stories come from the serendipitous meetings, navigating unexpected challenges, surprise performances at the eleventh hour. Great stories are after all about the journey, not the outcome.

11.

War Paint

Amy was one of my first preteen clients working with the horses at Two Bear. Her enthusiasm and curiosity vibrated off of her as she took in the surroundings of the interior of the barn. I could feel her itching to start firing off questions. Her mother Scarlett had approached me one evening after I gave a presentation to an organization that supported foster and adoption families in the area. Serendipitously, our lives had also overlapped years previously through Pikes Peak Therapeutic Riding Center in Colorado Springs, where I first began my supervision with the other therapists Jody and Rita. Scarlett had taken her kids to PPTRC for adaptive riding lessons before they had relocated to Montana. During those last years in Colorado, she and her husband had fostered and later adopted three children who had a particularly difficult upbringing. As the oldest sibling of those kids, Amy came across as a typical horse-loving teenager at first glance, but her bright blue eyes betrayed a history of abandonment and emotional trauma. She and her siblings were frequently homeless with drug-addicted and unavailable parents and living out of the family car. Leaving to go score or use, they left eight-year-old Amy with the responsibility of caring for her two younger siblings, one of whom was still in diapers. Despite the adoption and separation from her biological parents, Amy still felt the burden of her role as the caregiver to her siblings. Scarlett and her husband wanted her to release the expectations she held of herself in order to enjoy the childhood that had been previously taken from her.

Amy was now a preteen who happened to be obsessed with horses and her mother was hopeful that through that fascination, some healing could take place in our sessions. We worked together learning horsemanship, managing communication at home, fostering her dreams and creativity. She worked extensively on drawings with the finest detail that she would often bring to her sessions, or showcase a new pair of riding boots or book on horses, glowing with pride.

After taking the long Montana winter off from working together, Amy's mother Scarlett reached out to continue our equine sessions for the remainder of that summer. Stepping out of the family car, Amy was tall, lithe and lanky. I had become used to most 14-year-olds towering over me, but I was stunned by her growth spurt. With her thick, red hair swept back in a swishing ponytail, she was starting to look more mature and blossoming into a young woman. Scarlett had called me prior to one of our sessions with concern of Amy's recent behavior at her weekly youth group, where she had started flirting with a boy and acting in a way to bring more attention towards herself.

Amy was quite adept at horsemanship skills by this point and I pushed her to work at liberty with a horse in the round pen just below the horse pasture. The tall, slanted walls enclosed us in privacy but left the views of horses, mountains and the vast sky uninhibited. Those high wooden walls radiated heat from the sun above and provided a private nook encasing the three of us. Teenagers, naturally pushing away from their parents and making forays into independence, are in need of mentors and role models who help them navigate their changing roles and identity, but in a safe space where they can also be direct.

Knowing Amy may become embarrassed by the uncomfortable topic and wanting to respect her family's values, I paused, choosing my words carefully. "Look, you're going to want boys to notice you, that's completely normal. But I don't want you changing who you are, what you like, how you dress, trying to get their attention."

This seemed to resonate with her as she paused, processing the information while untangling the horse's mane with her fingers. "That makes sense," she said after a minute.

Smiling to break the seriousness between us, I softened, "You want someone who is drawn to the already wonderful attributes about you."

Navigating the discrepancies between family values and innate developmental changes can feel confusing and impossible to teenage girls if we don't help create a realistic road map for them. We are only doing them a disservice if we don't help them develop positive ways in wanting to draw a new type of attention towards themselves. Cringing from our own pasts, we might remember our first attempts at flirting where we may have tried to make ourselves diminutive by acting helpless, dressing provocatively, taking on the interests and hobbies of our crush, or talking negatively about our female peers in comparison. A mentor or older peer can normalize the changing behaviors and desire to be noticed by reinforcing the most effective and healthy strategy of remaining true to themselves and highlighting their own strengths and interests.

Later that summer, on a hot afternoon when standing in the sun or lots of movement felt unbearable, I tied our white horse Yogo in the shade of the barn. I set out two cups, one full of sidewalk chalk and the other with water. From under the brim of my large straw hat, I told Amy how we could wet the chalk to draw on our horse and gave her two options for an activity. She could either use one side of the horse's body to represent her past and the other side as her future, or she could create symbols that represented her strengths and attributes that she liked most about herself. I explained how in indigenous horse cultures, warriors would depict their horses with dots, lightning bolts, circles and other symbols to represent the rider's skill and accomplishments. Like every other girl her age, Amy didn't hesitate in picking the war paint option. I loved how girls at this age were still unabashed in being able to compliment themselves and note their strengths without being overly humble or dismissive.

I watched as she hesitatingly experimented with the chalk, testing different shades on Yogo's creamy white coat, dipping them in the water, and twisting her mouth in concentration before drawing her first symbol. A blue flower on a stem emerged on his flank, then stick figures on his shoulder, a red heart on his barrel and streaks of alternating colors in his mane. A yellow sun illuminated her art from above on Yogo's back and she began coloring her hand with hot-pink chalk, before stamping in on his shoulder twice, much like a signature to her final work.

I asked Amy to tell me about each of the symbols and wasn't surprised by her answers, having heard many of them before from other girls her age. She spoke of having a large heart and being a good friend to others. The flower represented her love for animals and nature, caring for her dogs, goats and chickens at home and dreaming of a career with animals. She felt the strength of her family and was able to feel gratitude for her life like the warmth of the sun, despite the several years of her troubled and unstable past that she worked hard to forget.

I loved spending time with the other adolescent girls like Amy. They were so full of kindness and compassion for others, struggling with their tendencies towards inner reflection and solitude in nature. They were just transitioning into the age where they started noticing the subtle differences between themselves and their peers, but young enough to refrain from the pressure to change or alter themselves.

Noticing the pink, blue and orange highlights in Yogo's mane, I asked Amy what they represented. "I'm not sure," she shrugged.

As her therapist, I pressed her slightly to consider that those highlights weren't entirely coincidental. Amy had just turned 14 and I knew that was a typical age where girls started receiving special privileges like cell phone use, later bedtimes or simple makeup. Being the eldest girl in a fairly conservative household, her parents hadn't completely decided which makeup she would be allowed to begin experimenting with, but it sounded like lip gloss and mascara for special occasions. I suggested that the highlights were a simple act of self-expression and creativity, much like the choices we make with our own appearance. We talked about some of the practicalities with makeup use and application. I felt honored to witness a rite-of-passage that I believe holds a much deeper message for us as women.

I remembered with a twinge of embarrassment the early experiments with the makeup I found in my mother's and older sister's drawers; foundations several shades off, different shades of lip color and vibrant eyeshadow. *What was I thinking?* We don't always have a guide to help us select appropriate or flattering colors, or someone to remind us that we were highlighting the beauty that already existed, not hiding it. When I turned 13, my mother had gifted me an introductory makeup consultation at a department store. I remember feeling so supported by both my mother and the esthetician. It was such an intimate experience to have someone apply lip color and shadow to my eyelids, waiting with anticipation to see the final results in the handheld mirror. Women have been using style, color and shape for centuries for our self-expression and identity. At times we may not have held a voice, our lips were still painted red.

I found it fitting that Amy's parents had allowed her to highlight her lips and her eyes. I wanted her to reflect on how she could use her voice and the eyes in which she saw the world as she stepped into her journey as a woman. Like many of the other adolescent girls who were drawn to the therapeutic nature of horses, Amy held the weight of a difficult past that she struggled to find meaning in. She was denied the care and protection most children should receive and was passed back and forth between her biological family and adoptive parents as the court system determined her fate each time. She minimized her needs with her adoptive family with her child mind reasoning that if she took up less space, her adoptive parents would not see her as a burden and decide to keep her.

Her family now wanted Amy to address the old fear of being a burden by using her voice to advocate for herself, freely and without hesitation. When the snow began to fly that next winter, Amy transitioned out of our weekly sessions. Like most therapy clients who have met their goals during our time together, we soon lost touch. But knowing that same buzzing vibrational spark she carried during our first interaction, I know she is excelling at whatever she directs that energy towards.

I have worked with many adult women who have unfortunately lost that voice and cowered from drawing any attention to themselves. Throughout our sessions, they would reflect on how years of not caring about their appearance had lowered their self-esteem. They felt overwhelmed trying to find flattering clothes, a new hairstyle or felt foolish wearing makeup. Cautioning them that any sense of adorning themselves was personal and strictly for themselves, not to look like an algorithm or the women they saw idolized on social media, we would start small. Wear perfume one day. Find a new piece of clothing that feels comfortable and soothing when you wear it. Remove clothing from your closet that reminds you of the weight you intend to lose or that feels like a costume for an inauthentic version of yourself.

Beauty is the opposite of practicality, but we have been enchanted by it for centuries. I hoped that young girls like Amy would see that theirs extended much deeper below their skin; the art and drawings they spent hours on, speaking up for a classmate, hearts breaking at the injustices they saw in the world, sharing their hobbies and talents, applauding the gifts of others and dreaming of big futures for themselves.

Horses are born with dozens of variations of coat and mane colors and markings; each one more stunning than the last. My favorite, the dapple grey, consists of a striking dark-grey webbing over a lighter grey coat. But anyone who has owned a white or grey horse knows they have one particularly annoying habit; they like to get dirty. These horses, despite their startling beauty and uniqueness, have through evolution internalized that they stand out. Standing out makes them a more visible target to predators, so they will roll in the dirt and mud to conform better to the variations of their brown, black and beige herd mates. Like conforming to the herds of middle school, young girls are hoping to deflect unnecessary attention directed towards themselves. At another end of the spectrum, those who have endured physical or sexual abuse tend to minimize or alter their appearance in an attempt to not stand out as well.

I frequently encounter clients who are recovering from an abusive or controlling relationship, leaving the client struggling with their self-esteem, self-worth and perception of reality. Someone who has narcissistic traits strategically presents themselves to a vulnerable and easily impressionable person and, slowly over time, pushes boundaries and inflicts more emotional damage. One of the most common ways that a narcissist controls their target is by diminishing their perception of self and self-image. It can start as subtle as, "You're going to wear that?" Or "I like it when you do your makeup this way."

The comments extend deeper beyond physical appearance. I once worked with a woman whose previous partner used to downplay her cooking skills and tell others that he was the chef in the relationship, despite the fact that she had graduated from culinary school and owned her own bakery. A common tactic a manipulator may use is triangulation, meant to draw comparisons between their victim and another person with opposing traits; the socialite, the blonde, the fitness junkie. Now with a false enemy, the victim directs their attention trying to shape themselves to be more like their opposite to maintain the attraction of the person with narcissistic traits. When our self-worth is contingent upon the approval of others, we lose the freedom of being our authentic and more beautiful selves.

For those who unfortunately found an abusive or unhealthy relationship early on in their dating life, the climb away from unhealthy relationships can be a lengthy journey, as their sense of a normal relationship is skewed. A new partner who subtly inflicts emotional damage is a vast improvement from someone who was blatantly abusive, but still a far cry from a partner who is confident in themselves and celebrates the unique traits of their partner.

Beth had grown up in a chaotic household, where neither parent was present or available to provide basic care, let alone emotional attention. Eager to leave home but without any family or financial support, Beth started living with a boyfriend while she was completing her college courses. Her boyfriend, hot-tempered and manipulative, loved to toy with her emotions by crudely commenting on other women's bodies and openly having sexual affairs. Knowing that Beth relied on splitting rent to pay for her courses, her partner had her trapped in a powerless situation. Despite his salacious behavior, her boyfriend would become enraged at any attention Beth received from others and began picking out her outfits, which were meant to be humiliating and unflattering. After nearly two years of physical and emotional abuse, Beth was able to move out and began supporting herself in her new career, where she quickly met and started dating a coworker.

In our therapy sessions, Beth began addressing previous trauma and the ways she had worked to deflect attention towards herself—her lack of social life, not caring for her body or home and a closet full of clothes that didn't feel like herself. Her new relationship provided stability and encouragement, as she began making new friends, finding routines that built on caring for herself, and playing with her sense of style. Beth made enormous growth professionally and personally before her world was upended when her new boyfriend broke up with her after ten months. She worked at putting the pieces of her life back together while nursing hurt emotions, before she made two fortunate connections with women who became role models, taking her under their wings.

In one of our final therapy sessions, Beth was eager to disclose an epiphany she recently had, recognizing her last boyfriend had not been the incredible partner she had initially imagined. His compliments reflected a desire to shape her choices rather than praise her, and he too created jealousy between Beth and other female coworkers. Beth amazed me with her acceptance and gratitude that he had served a role in her life when she needed that reassurance. But now that his role was complete, she was looking forward to meeting a partner who continued to build her up and accept her wholeheartedly for the genuine version of herself.

It can feel especially vulnerable to showcase our sense of style, accomplishments, talents, or stories, after we have falsely been misled to believe it creates unwanted attention. We avert our gaze, apologize and minimize, much like the grey horses who cover themselves with mud and dust. Our society for too long has profited off of women chasing impossible beauty standards in the quest for finding what they 'should' look like. We have the opportunity to build and educate future generations on the power they hold in how they choose to represent and express themselves. Beth was fortunate to have two women notice the need to uplift and encourage her efforts, while Amy was blessed with parents who wanted to encourage her confident beauty before she began entertaining dating. Like the jagged lightning bolts and symbols depicted on the flanks of brave horses, our adversities can be worn with pride for having navigated and survived them. Our histories give us strength and courage, making us unique and beautiful.

12.

Seeking Congruence in the Herd

As an equine therapist I am honored to carry the bruises of my past as their own form of war paint to share with clients. And in comparing our stories, I'm greatly humbled in the abundance of blessings I too often take for granted—supportive friends and family, a safe home, opportunities to grow and chase my passion. Each client I have encountered is unique with a remarkable set of circumstances that have led them to where they are in that moment. Whether in an office or in the stillness of a barn, therapy provides the space to hold the heaviness of life while reminding us that we are never alone. It is an honor to be invited in to so many rich and diverse stories. When exploring how past experiences have shaped the way they view themselves and the world around them, I will invite a client to create a timeline of their major life events. They can map out the 'high points' and 'low points' for a visual representation and together, we comb through looking for the narratives they have internalized as a result of those events.

Much like from my own past, the most common narrative we combat is the 'I'm not good enough' belief. Similarly, 'I am bad' can be a false internalized narrative from childhood abuse or 'I am helpless' can originate from feeling stuck or trapped in various circumstances. We grieve how those false narratives have held us back, a heavy weight we have carried for years or decades even. And then, in a long, but deliberate process, those beliefs are replaced with positive or neutral ones. We may extend forgiveness to ourselves or others, or hold a larger perspective for the hidden blessings those events may have indirectly led to. It is human nature to consider whether the internalized view of ourself is accurately mirrored back through our interactions and relationships with others. In a world inundated with outside influence, it has become more difficult to find congruence between the two, but also more necessary. Finding that sense of congruence within ourselves will inevitably lead to embracing the larger role that we serve.

Not all clients who seek out equine therapy are horse people, but they all know the clarity that sitting in the stillness of nature provides or the thrill that chasing the wildness reignites. That wildness instills a sense a belonging, a community based in the resiliency that only nature provides. With that same childlike wonder that built forts under tree branches and climbed over fences into the neighbor's horse pasture, I extend that curiosity

232

into the hours with my clients. Reconnecting with the natural world around us reinvigorates that sense of play and wonderment. With hearts thumping with adrenaline, it is intoxicating to feel small and held in the vastness of the universe, reminding ourselves how miraculous it is to be alive in a world that interacts back.

The romanticism of the American West has pulled millions of lonely hearts to the lap of the mountains, hoping the magic of their proximity may soothe the brokenness inside us. I was born in the dry summer heat of the plains, under the protective gaze of the Rockies, and have spent much of my life since fighting between the innate need to return home and the external temptation of considering another lifestyle. Those same fingers that hungrily reached through the neighbor's fence to touch the horse were perhaps the same wildness that compelled those first few humans who dipped their fingers in the ochre paints and scrawled a likeness of the ancient equine on the prehistoric cave walls of Lascaux in southwestern France. Perhaps it is the remnants of our primitive nature, when man first observed the wild horse herds and recognized a reciprocal need that could only be met through one another. The unspoken language of Equus has mystically united horse and human for eons, but for some of us, it is a music we cannot ignore.

The cohesion within communities and our social circles is largely due to the balance of interpersonal dynamics that exist between all members. Finding which role we play within our families, friends and coworkers is an ongoing and deliberate process. We will always be pulled and shifted by outside influence, but the never-ending search for purpose is what ultimately grounds us during our time on earth. Moving and changing scenery has tempted me with the enormity of lives one can possibly lead. Whenever I find myself with horses, I'm my most authentic myself—a dreamer with a featherlight heart, lifted with possibilities, yet humbled and grateful for each miraculous moment I experience with these sensitive, wise and powerful creatures.

Within a herd, each horse plays an integral role in the safety and maintenance of the group cohesion. Structure and familiarity of herd roles creates peace for the herd members, where conflicts are resolved quickly and routine provides a feeling of safety and a quiet understanding permeates between each horse. Stepping into a well-established herd that peace descends upon me and my clients, so long as we respect the space and read each horse's level of tolerance, we are welcomed to participate. Horses for me were a needed refuge of acceptance in times of trouble, hurt and heartache. My vocation is to extend that ripple of peace into as many lives as I encounter, both in the barn and in my therapy office. Much like horses, the routines and connections anchor me, staving off the fears of uncertainty. For horses do not dread tomorrow, they do not ruminate in the painful injustices they have suffered. They learn and they can anticipate, but they live wholly in the moment, observing, savoring.

In a balanced herd of both male and female horses, there is the alpha male who protects the herd from outside threats, but there is also an alpha female who guards the integrity of internal herd dynamics through her calm wisdom. I saw this best exemplified in the herd of Two Bear horses in Montana between Whiskey and Sparkle. Whiskey, despite his smaller stature and being one of the senior members, was an exemplary alpha male. His leadership was so ingrained into the herd that I rarely saw him reprimand another horse; no one was willing to challenge him or step out of line, and peace persisted in the herd. When the matriarchal Sparkle was removed from the pasture for a therapeutic riding lesson however, the other horses would whinny in distress, calling for her to respond the entire hour she was missing, until she was returned to them. Most humans and animals prefer emotional comfort and safety, negating even physiological needs, such as feeding. When Sparkle's nurturing and confident presence was returned to the pasture, the other horses would each wait to greet her individually with their noses outstretched, before huffing a giant sigh of relief, shaking the tension from their necks, and resume licking and chewing with a restored lowered head. Neither Whiskey or Sparkle ever showed distress themselves when they were removed from the herd. They were confident in their role both within the horse herd and in the larger herd of our organization as they served in lessons. The women of Two Bear had worked diligently to reinforce their role of a compassionate and capable leader to these alpha horses while they were in our care. Each horse in return offered the reliability of their role.

It is said that a therapist can only take a client as far as they themselves have gone, and I know I'm still rapidly evolving with plenty of life lessons headed my direction. Perhaps if I'm patient enough that next lesson of Equus will begin to reveal itself in time. Tucker, who doesn't share my keenness for horses, faithfully follows my every footfall. His now whitened face and developing arthritis can't mask his enthusiasm for greeting each person he encounters.

I know I have found a once-in-a-lifetime companion in Tucker and I'm soothed thinking of the brief but lasting impact he has played in so many lives, grateful for each new day with him. I remember years ago, while living and working in Colorado, I took the two of us up high into the mountains near

Guanella Pass, where we could hike together off-leash above the treeline. After a full afternoon exploring the alpine lakes and Tucker following the loose scent trails of various critters, we began our descent back to the trailhead when a lone figure appeared on the path headed in our direction. The wind is constant at that elevation of 12,000 feet, and I hadn't heard the man approaching in time to leash Tucker, who was galloping the hundred yards in his direction. "Is this Tucker from Mustard Seed?" the man called out excitedly. More than two hours from home, high in the wilderness, Tucker was still recognizable for his enthusiastic greeting. We can never underestimate the power in making someone feel seen, however fleeting.

I'm fortunate to have a tolerant dog, who is able to ignore the frequent moves I put him through, so long as he finds himself included in all the transitions. I hope this can be the move that settles me and the boxes I have been storing for years can be off-handed for someone else to use. Having moved 14 times in 14 years, I'm hoping to finally unpack, literally and metaphorically. Much like finding congruence in the external environment around me, I believe finding congruence within myself is the next lesson I have yet to fully reconcile.

Like the prayer flags offering their blessings to the wind, in wishing for myself, I must also extend that wish to others.

My wish would be that each of us could connect, even for a moment, with that inner child within each of us. Whether in reflecting on our passions, the role in which we serve, a sense of curiosity and wonder or the purity of an innate sense of justice for others. The best gift we can give ourselves is an attempt at a childhood dream. Before the heartaches and limitations led us down a differing path, we ran barefoot with our arms flung wide open, our soul bravely pressed against the world. Aligning with our younger self, even for an hour of play, can recalibrate that genuine inner compass. While many nights I feel lost searching for that next big step, as long as I'm in the Rocky Mountains, close to the sound of hoofbeats, I know I am home.

Acknowledgements

This book could not have been made possible without the help and support of so many. I would like to thank my editor, Britt Collins, for her patient expertise and guidance in strengthening my voice. To Sinuhe Xavier, who encouraged me throughout the years of writing and for graciously lending his artistic talent to capture such a powerful cover image. A special thank-you to the Fort Lowell Neighborhood Association in Tuscon, Arizona in lending the Historic San Pedro Chapel for the location of the cover image. To Elly Nolen and her horse, Robin, whose extraordinary grace and patience made an ideal equine model. And to Victoria Walter and Mark Frank, for reading the earliest drafts and always believing in the horse girl.

About the Author

Emily Swisher is a licensed psychotherapist specializing in both equine interventions and trauma. Her education includes a Bachelor's of Science in Psychology from Colorado State University and a Master's in Clinical Counseling from Regis University. Additionally, Emily is a Certified Therapeutic Riding Instructor and Equine Specialist in Mental Health and Learning through PATH International. Her further interest in mind-body responses to trauma prompted her to become trained and certified in Eye Movement Desensitization and Reprocessing (EMDR). With her expertise in trauma and equine interventions, Emily has written several publications and spoken at conferences on trauma informed care in therapeutic riding facilities. She and her dog Tucker currently live in northwest Montana near the herd of Two Bear Therapeutic Riding Center.

For more information on upcoming events or to contact Emily, please visit www.emilyswishercounseling.com

Made in the USA
Middletown, DE
29 December 2024

68363951R00135